Having worked closely with Ben Sawatsky for severa with God" is not theory but reality in Ben's life. I am using this wonderful book as a daily devotional adventure with the Holy Spirit and my need to depend on Him for empowerment in all areas of life. Thank you, Ben, for sharing your journey with us!

William J. Hamel
President, Evangelical Free Church of America

Ben Sawatsky has been a wonderful friend and an effective ministry colleague for a number of years. It has been a joy to witness Ben's intimate walk with God. I believe that the Lord will use this engaging and practical book to encourage and help many of us to draw nearer to Jesus Christ and to enjoy a deeper intimacy with Him. I prayerfully recommend it to you.

Dr. Paul Cedar
Chairman, Mission America Coalition; Former President,
Evangelical Free Church of America

Few devotional books inspire an intimate walk with the Lord so fully and insightfully as this book. What makes this unique and distinctive is the way it radiates a personal walk with God. Ben Sawatsky shares his heart, and it reveals his own lifelong pilgrimage of walking in intimacy with His Majesty. You will find his insights regarding the Holy Spirit, prayer, and a quiet time helpful in your own pursuit of God.

Dr. Thomas A. McDill
Past President of the Evangelical Free Church of America

The greatest commandment is "to love God with our whole being." Dr. Benjamin Sawatsky, a man of God with a shepherd's heart, in his book *Intimacy with God* helps us know how to do that as he himself has lived this life. Filled with excellent exegesis and heartfelt prayers, Dr. Sawatsky leads us into developing intimacy with God through our relationship with the Holy Spirit, through our personal prayers, and through our quiet time. I heartily recommend this book to anyone wanting to get close and intimate with God.

Rev. Wilson A. Baria
National Director, Logos Wholistic Ministries, India

I read *Intimacy With God: Drawing Ever Closer to the Almighty* with joy! I am so pleased that a book on intimacy with God, written by an outstanding evangelical leader, would be rooted upon a solid biblical reflection on the work of the Holy Spirit! And what moved me most is that it comes from the heart of a man who is committed to knowing God!

Rev. Edmund Chan
Leadership-Mentor, Covenant Evangelical Free Church, Singapore

My life has been repeatedly challenged toward a more intimate walk with God through Ben's life and writings. But as I watched these documents emerge monthly over a number of years, I was particularly impressed with how our missionaries around the world were deeply touched and motivated toward the closer walk with God. I pray that these essays will now stimulate many more to seek an intimate walk with the Almighty.

Dr. Thomas Cairns
Former Associate Executive Director for International Ministries,
EFCA International Mission

This book will inspire a diligent pursuit of an intimate walk with God. Dr. Sawatsky has shared transparently his own growing relationship with God through the Holy Spirit. His book is a "must read" for all cross-cultural missionaries who hunger for intimacy with the Almighty. Many will view it as a manual for intimacy with God.

Rev. Robert Dillon
Former Executive Director, Evangelical Free Church Mission

In knowing Ben Sawatsky for almost fifty years and having worked with him for over ten years, I have observed a man who demonstrates a life of "Intimacy with God." The prayers in this book have greatly enriched my personal devotional life. I highly recommend this book to anyone desiring a closer walk with God.

Rev. Jim Forstrom
Former Associate Executive Director,
EFCA International Mission

This book arises from a lifetime of walking under the Lordship of Jesus Christ. The author, with whom I have worked for over four decades, has progressively experienced the sanctifying hand of the Holy Spirit in his life. You will see evidence of this on practically every page. It is a unique book, and one you will not soon forget. I commend it to all who welcome a deeper walk with God through Jesus Christ and in the power of the Holy Spirit.

Dr. Allen Tunberg
Former Asia Director for the EFCA International Mission

Intimacy with God

Drawing Ever Closer to the Almighty

Dr. Benjamin A. Sawatsky

BookVillages

Intimacy with God: Drawing Ever Closer to the Almighty

© 2011 by Benjamin A Sawatsky

ISBN-13: 978-0-98371-701-0

Cover and interior design by Niddy Griddy Design, Inc.

Cover photo by Dr. Benjamin A. Sawatsky

Cover and interior illustration © iStock

LCCN: 2011911372

Printed in the United States of America

15 14 13 12 11   1 2 3 4 5 6 7 8

Dedication

I dedicate this book on intimacy with God

to my dear wife, Muriel,

to my son, Kevin, and his wife, Rene,

to my daughter, Kimberly,

and to my four grandchildren—Benjamin, Michaela,

Kinsleigh, and Austin.

CONTENTS

FOREWORD

In 1995 I was given the opportunity to travel to India with Dr. Benjamin Sawatsky, the executive director of the Evangelical Free Church Mission. I had never met Ben—our "vision trip" group actually met for the first time at Seattle International Airport before we flew to Tokyo, then to Thailand for an overnight stop before we flew on to India. The following morning Ben assembled us for a strategy and prayer meeting where he shared what our seventeen days would include, in addition to the fourteen plane flights scheduled. Yes, fourteen!

I remember asking Ben, "What are your expectations for us as a team?" We had come from a dozen different churches, were mostly senior pastors or missions directors, and all were in some way connected with the Free Church's new work in India. I'll never forget Ben's answer, which evidently was his standard one: "Be prepared at any moment to preach, sing, or die." Wow. Here was someone I wanted to know—and follow!

In 1999 I was elected for the first time to the national board of what was then the Evangelical Free Church Mission, but soon thereafter became the EFCA-IM, or International Mission. It was around that same time that Ben began to write his essays on "Intimacy with God," the very threads of which have been woven into this book. They were written and distributed to the far-flung family of missionaries serving in over thirty countries, and we as board members were happily included in each monthly transmission.

I'm not sure if it was in the second or third month of receiving these small gems of deep spiritual insight that I thought, "This should be a book." I know I said the same thing to Ben within the first year of his writing them. Two years later, I was elected the chair of the mission board, a position I held for the last three years of Ben's term as executive director, and the first year with T.J. Addington in that position. Ben continued to write, and I continued to cheer and to believe that this was something that our broader church family needed to read. Ben and I even had a few conversations on-the-fly about the "Intimacy with God" pieces at the time of his retirement. But with his new title of Global Ambassador for ReachGlobal (the current name of the EFCA mission) he was looking forward, not back to work which was at that time several years in the rearview mirror.

And then came a chilling diagnosis of several symptoms Ben was experiencing: Alzheimer's. To say that it stunned a significant portion of the missionary world is probably not an overstatement. This man, so vital into his sixth and seventh decades, renowned for his sharp mind, his passion for the lost, his incredible personal disciplines, his care of his earthly frame—how could it be that God would allow Ben to lose any portion of that?

We prayed. We cried. We comforted ourselves by knowing that even then, a "Well done, good and faithful servant" was secured—but we also railed against God, if truth be told. And I personally grieved that Ben's "Intimacy with God" essays might never see the light of day of larger distribution.

Our God is still a God of miracles, though, isn't He? He delights in confounding His critics, answering prayers, restoring the sight of the blind, allowing the lame to leap, the deaf to hear—and for some inexplicable, unbelievable, miraculous reason, God did something in Ben's life. Either God healed Ben of Alzheimer's, or He put him into some kind of remission for a season—but suddenly Ben was "back." His mind was clearing, his passions were re-energized, and all things seemed possible again.

And so we got busy. When I say "we" I mean Ben, of course, and two of his dearest friends—Dr. Tom Cairns and Jim Forstrom, who have walked the life of faith with Ben for years—and me. I perhaps elbowed my way into this quartet, offering to help reformat and simplify and prepare for printing what you hold in your hands, because I believed, and believe, so strongly in what these essays signify. And we worked quickly. Just as all of us who await with expectation the soon-coming return of Jesus, there are also times to hurry a project to completion. We worked and prayed and conferred and re-worked, trusting that God's Holy Spirit—the very centrality of each essay—would be the Overseer of the project. He was. He did.

So what you have waiting as a gift to unwrap is a true collaboration. But the collaboration is not of men and women doing anything of import—it is the collaborative work of the Holy Spirit of the Risen Christ, continuing "to perfect until the day of Christ Jesus" one very yielded heart and soul. What Ben has done through these writings is to allow us a small window into the world of a true lover of Jesus as he humbly and intentionally seeks to go daily deeper in intimacy with the living God.

I think one could read this book two ways. First, it could be read as an interesting, even inspiring picture of one man's spiritual intersections with Emmanuel. There might be plenty to encourage or exhort you along the way. But if instead it is read with an open heart, asking the Holy Spirit to interpret each principle, make each Scripture personal, to allow Him with all humility and openness to have free rein? Ah, that is exactly what Ben would want. And what Tom, Tim, Jim, Al, and I would rejoice over as well.

Jenni Key
June, 2011

PREFACE

For me, there is both personal and Mission history behind the well-known phrase, *Intimacy with God.*

In December of 1997, I was urged by our Moscow-based workers to join them in discussions regarding alarming developments in Russia's Duma (Parliament). Emerging legislation pointed to most, if not all, of our international staff facing imminent expulsion. Our future in Russia was precarious, like a heavy weight suspended by a single thread. But praise be to our sovereign God, since He had woven the thread, we were secure in His eternal purposes. Nevertheless, our country leader, Kevin DeVera, overcame my reluctance to cut short our vacation in the north woods of Wisconsin to join our staff for discussions in Moscow.

Our workers assigned Pastor Noah Palmer, mission board member and travel companion, to stay with me in Jim and Lois McNeil's vacant apartment. The subzero temperatures and abundance of piled snow everywhere was typical of Moscow in December. The discussions were very profitable. But totally unknown to me, my sovereign Lord had yet another agenda item to bring to my attention. I was soon to learn that my coming to Moscow had more to do with my walk with God than the proceedings in the Russian Duma.

In the middle of one of the five nights in Moscow, I was awakened by what seemed like a voice asking simply, *"Will you walk more closely with Me?"* I answered in the affirmative and immediately fell back into a deep sleep. Awhile later I heard the same "voice" asking the same question, *"Will you walk more closely with Me?"*

This repeat of the same question awakened me completely. In my heart I knew that this was the Holy Spirit nudging me toward a closer walk with God. I was not afraid or curious, but neither did I know where this intensified pursuit of intimacy with God would take me.

Once back in Minneapolis, I cleared my desk and computer of a sizeable list of important matters needing my attention. Muriel flew to San Diego ahead of me to prepare for Christmas celebrations with our daughter, Kimberly. I intended to take with me a book on the history of Uzbekistan to read over the holidays. I could not find it, but instead my eyes fell on J. Oswald Sanders's book entitled *Enjoying Intimacy with God.*

Over the following weeks I noticed with delight a growing hunger for time alone in the presence of God—more time in the Scriptures and more time in prayer. The Holy Spirit was helping me to make good my commitment a few weeks earlier in Moscow.

For a period of over twelve years leading the Mission, I wrote a monthly four-page memo to the family of missionaries of the Evangelical Free Church of America International Mission. In January 1998 I began to write the earliest essays on intimacy with God—only a month after my Moscow trip. I felt *compelled* to share thoughts on intimacy with God with the members of our growing staff of international workers. Most of the essays noted in the table of contents reflect an edited version of essays on this topic.

Now in retirement, I can see the fruit of the Moscow encounter with my Lord. It wasn't long before I perceived a subtle but clear shift in my leadership focus. I was at the halfway point in my twelve years as executive director of the Mission. I see the first six years as focused on strategic planning and vision casting. These two emphases were both enjoyable and essential, but the Holy Spirit's prompting in Moscow underscored the need for greater balance in my kingdom leadership. If the operative word the first six years was *strategic*, it shifted more to the *relational* during the final six years—my relationship with my sovereign Lord and with my fellow kingdom workers. I embraced the truth that what my fellow missionaries needed most from me was a personal, intimate walk with God.

Finally, since this book is a book on intimacy with God, I must leave you with a working definition and two questions to ponder. I came to define *intimacy with God* as "going progressively deeper in knowing God, loving God, and serving God."

The questions are: How can we possibly love the God we do not know intimately? And, how can we long serve the God we do not love with all of our heart, soul, mind, and strength?

Dr. Benjamin A. Sawatsky
June, 2011

ACKNOWLEDGMENTS

Everyone knows that a team is more productive than a "lone-ranger-leader." The project team for this book is no exception. I needed the professional help given so sacrificially by T.J. Addington, Thomas Cairns, Jenni Key, James Forstrom, and Allen Tunberg. Specifically, the members of the project team did the following:

- Introduced our book to the publisher;
- Wove the essays and prayers into a cohesive book;
- Proofed the master manuscript multiple times;
- Engaged in prayer for the Holy Spirit's anointing of the book.

A Thousand Thanks to the Project Team!

SECTION I

Intimacy with God
and
the Holy Spirit

THE HOLY SPIRIT AS MY COMFORTING COUNSELOR

My goal in this series of essays on the Holy Spirit and intimacy with God is to demonstrate from Scripture that there is nothing of eternal significance that we can accomplish without the help of the Holy Spirit. Our sovereign Lord made this convincingly clear when He had Zechariah say to Governor Zerubbabel regarding the rebuilding of the temple: *"Not by might nor by power, but by my Spirit," says the LORD Almighty* (Zechariah 4:6). And so it is with any kingdom initiative today. He will fulfill all of His eternal purposes. He will do so by His Spirit.

What do we mean by intimacy with God? Intimacy with God is a diligent pursuit of going progressively deeper in knowing, loving, and serving God. The intentional choice of the words *knowing, loving*, and *serving* reflect a prioritized order. Love for God flows out of knowing God, and service for God proceeds from loving God. We cannot truly love the God we do not know, and we certainly cannot serve with joy the God we do not love. (This, by the way, makes the Great Commandment to love God with all of our heart, soul, mind, and strength so critical to intimacy with God.) Both love and service for God are by-products of knowing God. To know Him is to love Him, and to love Him is to serve Him. The most urgent quest for the believer is to know God and then to love and serve Him.

The clear implication from our definition is that intimacy with God is a process, a lifelong process, a process we often refer to as progressive sanctification. Paul describes the journey toward intimacy with God in these words: *"Being confident of this, that he who began a good work in you will carry it on to completion until the day of Christ Jesus"* (Philippians 1:6).

> Intimacy with God is a process, a lifelong process.

Our most prominent example of a passionate pursuit of knowing Jesus Christ is the apostle Paul. Near the end of his illustrious missionary career, as a prisoner in chains, he reiterated his deepest desire to know Christ (Philippians 3:8,10). Paul's grand goal throughout his converted days was to grow steadily stronger in knowing Jesus Christ. This must also be the overarching goal of the twenty-first century believer.

Apart from the continuous help of the Holy Spirit, intimacy with God is wishful thinking—a literal impossibility. He is the One who mediates the conscious presence of God the Father and God the Son to us. Jesus promised the disciples that when He returned to the Father, He would send "another Counselor" in His place. The Greek word for the Holy Spirit is the *parakletos* which means "a person summoned to one's aid." The Holy Spirit has been sent by God the Father in answer to Jesus' prayer to come alongside every believer as his/her counselor, companion, comforter, encourager, and helper. He is the infinitely-wise counselor, the intimately-near companion, the calming comforter, the edifying encourager, and the tireless helper. What a rich list of terms describing the work of the Holy Spirit in us!

That we need the help of the Holy Spirit in our pursuit of an intimate walk with God is clear. The child of God desperately needs Him in every life and ministry situation. Consider the following:

- Do we set out to engage in _intercessory prayer?_ We need the help of the Holy Spirit to *aid* us in our praying as well as to *align* our prayers with the Father's eternal purposes.
- Do we propose to do the work of *evangelism?* This important ministry cannot be fruitful apart from the convicting work of the Holy Spirit. Left to ourselves, we will labor a lifetime without making even one convert. The Holy Spirit is the one who convicts the world of sin, of righteousness, and of judgment.

  H.S. Renewed me of Your Business & my call to pray for those in need

- Do we resolve to *build a convincing case* for Jesus Christ as the eternal Son of God among our friends who have dismissed His claims? Our most eloquent apologetic will not move a Buddhist, Hindu, Muslim, or post-modern secularist to follow Jesus Christ. The Holy Spirit takes our feeble words and builds a convincing case for Jesus.
- Are we in need of *guidance* in our missionary ministries? Only the Holy Spirit, the superintending guide of all missionary endeavors, can provide clear direction.
- Do we desire to gain *a stronger grasp of God's ways and purposes* as outlined in the Scriptures? The Holy Spirit gives us "eyes" to see, "ears" to hear, "minds" to comprehend, and "hearts" to obey. He instructs and tutors us in the Scriptures He Himself inspired human authors to write.
- Do we long for greater *Christlikeness* in our relationships? The Holy Spirit is the one who bears the attractive fruit.
- Are we in need of *comfort and hope* in the midst of an unbearably difficult situation? The Holy Spirit delights in coming alongside the believer as his/her comforting counselor to remove or administer strength for the difficult situations.

How wonderful and how indispensable is the work of the Holy Spirit in the life of the child of God! From morning till night, every day, the Holy

Spirit is engaged in the life and work of the Christian. He stands ready 24–7 to fill the role of comforting counselor in each of us.

"And I will ask the Father, and he will give you another Counselor to be with you forever—the Spirit of truth. The world cannot accept him, because it neither sees him nor knows him. But you know him, for he lives with you and will be in you. I will not leave you as orphans; I will come to you" (John 14:16-18).

Note first the context for Jesus' wonderfully rich teaching on the Holy Spirit. Most of Jesus' comforting words about the Holy Spirit were uttered in the Upper Room, mere hours before His arrest and crucifixion. It is significant that the apostle John, the one among the twelve apostles who had the most intimate relationship with Jesus, says more about the Holy Spirit than any of the other gospel writers. He saw a direct correlation between the work of the Holy Spirit and an intimate relationship with the Lord Jesus Christ.

The Upper Room scene opens with Jesus washing His disciples' feet (see John 13:1-17). Jesus' action astounded the disciples and silenced all but Peter. His band of followers all knew that occasionally out of appreciation and respect, the followers of a rabbi would wash their teacher's feet. However, never, ever would the teacher wash the feet of his pupils. That simply did not and must not happen. Jesus did wash His disciples' feet and in so doing left us an example of servant leadership to imitate (see John 13:15).

> The completion of the Great Commission would be utterly impossible apart from the energizing power of the Holy Spirit.

When Jesus informed His disciples that He would be leaving them, they were deeply distraught. The very thought of life without Jesus filled them with unbearable sorrow. It was into this sad state of mind that He first promised that He would ask the Father to send another Counselor to take His place. Jesus knew that without the Holy Spirit the disciples could not cope with all that would befall them. The completion of the Great Commission would be utterly impossible apart from the energizing power of the Holy Spirit.

Note the essence of Jesus' promise to His disciples about the comforting Counselor:

"I will ask the Father, and he will give you another Counselor . . ." (John 14:16).

Jesus promised that He would pray to the Father for another Counselor. We can be certain that the Father would hear and answer His Son's prayers. The implication is that as He had been the disciples' Counselor while on earth, the Holy Spirit would take His place as "another Counselor" when He returned to the Father. While He was with them, had Jesus spoken words of comfort? So would the Counselor! Had He taught His disciples with power and authority? So would the Counselor! Had Jesus rebuked His followers when they lapsed into seeking positions for themselves? So would the Counselor!

"Another Counselor to be with you forever" (John 14:16).

Jesus pledged His word that the Counselor, the Spirit of truth, would be with them forever. He would not come and go. There would never be a break in His presence with them; it would be continuous. The Counselor would be everywhere present at the same time. He would be the omnipresent Counselor. As Jesus had mediated the presence of the Father to the disciples, so the Counselor would make Jesus' presence real after His ascension.

"The world cannot accept him, because it neither sees him nor knows him" (John 14:17).

Jesus warned that His teaching about the Holy Spirit would seem as nonsense to the world. The Counselor would reside in His followers only. As the world was divided over Jesus' identity, so our generation would also be blind to the person of the Holy Spirit. He seems weird and even spooky to those outside Jesus' company of followers.

"He lives with you and will be in you" (John 14:17).

The Holy Spirit had been with the disciples every day throughout their time with Jesus. Their relationship with Him was about to change. The day was just around the corner when He would reside in them—empowering, directing, and transforming them.

"I will not leave you as orphans" (John 14:18).

Even though Jesus was leaving His disciples to return to the Father, through the coming of the comforting Counselor, there would be no interruption to His presence. Children whose parents have abandoned them become orphans. Jesus promised that after His departure, the disciples would not become helpless, friendless orphans. Instead He promised to make provision for them, the wonderful provision of the Holy Spirit as their comforting Counselor.

"I will come to you" (John 14:18).

When Jesus gave His disciples the Great Commission, He declared that He would be with them to the end of the age. How would this be possible since He returned to the right hand of the Father immediately after giving the Great Commission? The answer is both profound and simple. Jesus would come to His followers through the omnipresent Holy Spirit. To this day, the Holy Spirit mediates the intimate presence of Jesus to you and to me.

There is no indication that the disciples of Jesus pined for the bodily presence of Jesus after Pentecost. They had mourned and grieved the loss of Jesus after His arrest and crucifixion, but after the Resurrection, and especially after Pentecost when the Holy Spirit was given to Jesus' followers, there is no record of further grief over Jesus' bodily absence. Never once do we hear the disciples say, *"Oh, that Jesus was back!" "Oh, that I could talk to Jesus about this!" "Oh, that I could hear Jesus teach one more time!" "Oh, how I miss Jesus!" "I wonder what Jesus would do in this situation."* They need not ask the WWJD (What Would Jesus Do?) question. Through the promptings and nudgings of the comforting Counselor, they knew clearly what Jesus would do.

After Pentecost, the Holy Spirit was in Jesus' followers to make the presence of the Lord Jesus consciously real, to jog their short memories of Jesus' teaching, and to superintend the charting of a course to complete the Great Commission. Jesus' followers were so conscious of His presence that they no longer needed His bodily presence. The Holy Spirit's work among us today is the same as it was with the apostles after Pentecost. It is to make the presence of Jesus as consciously real as though He stood bodily in our midst. Now, do we understand that intimacy with God the Father and God the Son is possible only through the work of the omnipresent Holy Spirit in us?

Prayer

Holy Spirit of truth, You are my comforting Counselor, my heavenly Father's gift in answer to Jesus' prayer for another Counselor. You warm my heart with a strong sense of God's holy presence. You fill my days with the conscious, continual presence of the Father and the Son. Apart from You, dear Holy Spirit, I would be quite oblivious to God's nearness.

Dear comforting Counselor, in times of sorrow and suffering You speak into my soul words of assurance, hope, and peace. You enable me to keep going when life gets heavy.

You give me joy, liberty, power, and passion when I proclaim Your truth.

You fill my soul with affections for things above, my heart with a growing understanding of the Son's eternal agenda, and my mind with insights into the very Scriptures You inspired. I shall wait in prayer till I hear You speak through Your living and powerful Word. Let my hearing turn to listening and my listening to obedience.

Dear comforting Counselor, speak clearly to us. Come among us with wisdom from above, with unmistakably clear direction, and with Your enabling power. Fill our hearts with such a hunger for God the Father that only He can satisfy, and with such an intense soul-thirst that He alone can quench. Unleash among us a sweeping spiritual awakening in which we see both sin and holiness from Your perspective.

This is my prayer to the Father, through the Son, by the Holy Spirit. Amen.

THE HOLY SPIRIT AS MY RESIDENT RABBI

Who among us has not longed for a teacher to explain the Scriptures to us? I have, and so did the Ethiopian eunuch reading the book of Isaiah without understanding its meaning. Guided by the Holy Spirit, Philip, the evangelist, approached the Ethiopian with the question, *"Do you understand what you are reading"*? In his response, the Ethiopian echoed the deep desire of all of us: *"How can I unless someone explains it to me?"* (see Acts 8:26ff). As students of the Scriptures, we need a teacher to aid us in our understanding.

Jesus as the Disciples' "Resident Rabbi"

Jesus' ministry among us revolved around teaching, preaching, and healing. In His three-pronged ministry, His teaching is given the greatest prominence by the four Gospel writers. He taught the crowds in public settings and the Twelve in more private contexts. He taught indoors in the synagogues and by the Sea of Galilee. He taught informally as He walked from place to place with His disciples. These disciples were blessed to have their beloved Teacher with them continually. Day after day in every conceivable life situation, Jesus was with them as their Teacher. Little wonder Jesus' band of followers was distraught over His repeated reminder that He would be leaving them (Matthew 16:21).

The big question in their minds was, "Who could possibly take Jesus' place as their 'Resident Rabbi'?" (*Rabbi,* by the way, means "teacher" or "a great man" in Hebrew. When Mary recognized Jesus after His resurrection, she exclaimed, "Rabboni," which means "My Teacher.") The disciples as well as the crowds were captivated by Jesus' teaching. He taught with authority. He confounded and silenced His critics. Again and again He took His disciples aside privately to help them understand His teachings.

Wonderful as Jesus' teaching was, comparatively few actually heard it from His lips. With the coming of the Holy Spirit, Jesus' followers everywhere would have within them the Prompter and Interpreter of Jesus' teachings.

We must pause here to be reminded of the prominence given to Jesus' teaching ministry. His teaching sessions are mentioned more often than His miracles. He understood the absolute necessity of having followers who understood His mission. He persevered in spite of their slowness to "get it." A major part of His mission was to help the apostles understand a specific body of truth. How do we know this? Listen to what Jesus said to His disciples in the Upper Room just prior to His arrest and crucifixion: *"I no longer call you servants, because a servant does not know his master's business. Instead, I have called you friends,* for everything that I learned from my Father I have made known to you" (John 15:15, emphasis added). As their Teacher, Jesus had completed His entire "curriculum."

The teaching gift is further highlighted in the Great Commission itself. It is impossible to complete the Great Commission to make disciples of all people groups apart from teaching everything He had commanded His followers. "Everything" encompasses the whole Bible. This was also the apostle Paul's understanding of Jesus' assignment; he reminded the Ephesian elders whom he had taught for three years that he had not hesitated to declare to them the whole counsel of God (see

Acts 20:27). To make disciples, we must do three things: evangelize the lost, baptize converts in the name of the triune God, and teach Jesus' followers the whole body of truth as recorded and preserved in the Old and New Testaments.

"But the Counselor, the Holy Spirit, whom the Father will send in my name, will teach you all things and will remind you of everything I have said to you" (John 14:26).

The primary application of this wonderful text is to the apostles as human, but inspired, authors of Scripture. Humanly speaking, they could not possibly remember all Jesus had taught them. Furthermore, only that select body of truth sovereignly determined by God would become part of the Bible. We call this the doctrine of inspiration. In His work of inspiration, the Holy Spirit would jog the disciples' memories to recall all Jesus had taught; He would also tutor them in their understanding of Jesus' teaching.

The Holy Spirit's work of inspiration has been completed. We must not expect additional Scriptures. When it comes to the doctrine of inspiration, I am a cessationist; that is, in the Spirit's work of recording God's Word in the Scriptures, there is nothing further to add. We can rejoice in the Bible as a final and finished product.

In this essay, however, we are more concerned about the doctrine of illumination. *By illumination we mean the Holy Spirit's help given to all.* I believe, and our text confirms this, that the Holy Spirit continues His work of illumination in the life of every follower of Christ on a daily basis. Whereas the Holy Spirit's work of inspiration produced the Scriptures, His work of illumination helps us to understand and obey the Scriptures that have already been written.

In our first text (John 14:26) the Holy Spirit does two things: First, *"Teach you all things."* The Holy Spirit's teaching role is very comprehensive. He will help us understand the entire Bible. He sheds light on all inspired

Scripture, allowing us to comprehend and apply it. Of course, it goes without saying that we must be students of the Scriptures, allowing the Holy Spirit to do His work of illumination. We do not understand Scripture all at one time. We can say that our Teacher, our *Resident Rabbi,* progressively illuminates our minds to understand the Scriptures. This is my own experience. I understand ever so much more today than even a few years ago. On our part there must be diligence and discipline, and on His part, the Holy Spirit leads us to understand just what we need.

> The Holy Spirit leads us to understand just what we need.

"Remind you of everything I have said to you." Still on the teaching of illumination, the Holy Spirit will remind us of just the needed biblical truth at the right time. We must not think that Jesus' teaching was limited to what is recorded in the New Testament gospels. "Everything" here is inclusive of all of Scripture. Have we forgotten Jesus' post-resurrection words to the two Emmaus travelers? *"This is what I told you while I was still with you: Everything must be fulfilled that is written about me in the Law of Moses, the Prophets and the Psalms"* (Luke 24:44). When Jesus said this, the New Testament, including the gospels, had not yet been written.

Why is the Holy Spirit's work of illumination so important? Simply stated, the Bible is incomprehensible apart from the illuminating work of the Holy Spirit. Since the Scriptures reveal the mind of God, we need the help of God's Spirit; He knows God's mind. We come to know God more deeply and completely as we go deeper and deeper in our understanding of the Scriptures. Paul reminds us that *"the man without the Spirit does not accept the things that come from the Spirit of God, for they are foolishness to him, and he cannot understand them,* because they are spiritually discerned" (1 Corinthians 2:14, emphasis added). Of course, the unbeliever can understand some matters of history, some narratives, and perhaps some proverbs in the Bible, but only on a superficial level.

Without the Holy Spirit, he cannot comprehend the ways of God as revealed in the Scriptures.

"But when he, the Spirit of truth, comes, he will guide you into all truth. He will not speak on his own; he will speak only what he hears, and he will tell you what is yet to come. He will bring glory to me by taking what is mine and making it known to you. All that belongs to the Father is mine. That is why I said that the Spirit will take from what is mine and make it known to you" (John 16:13-15).

The primary application in our second text must also be to the Holy Spirit's work of inspiration, but there are also at least two illumination applications for us to consider: *"He [the Holy Spirit] will bring glory to me [Jesus Christ]."* It is important to be reminded that the work of the Holy Spirit is Christo-centric. All that the Holy Spirit does and says ultimately points to Jesus Christ. His work of illumination is no exception. In my times of daily communion with the Almighty, the Holy Spirit makes the truths of Scripture come alive; He mediates the presence of God to me.

"He will tell you what is yet to come." These words will not likely lead to foretelling the future, though they could do so. In most cases the illuminating work of the Holy Spirit has a very practical guidance application for the servant of the Lord. For example, during my time as executive director of the EFCA International Mission, I spoke often of "building the road we are walking on." I understood these words to speak of the Holy Spirit's guidance for the steps ahead. One of the wonderful fruits of illumination is divine guidance.

My favorite definition of vision is "insight into God's purpose." The "insight" in this simple definition of vision must come to me through the Holy Spirit. It may sound mystical to ask the Holy Spirit to "write vision onto my heart," but it is nothing more than looking to Him to impress His plans and strategies onto my heart. Did not God put the rebuilding of the wall around Jerusalem into Nehemiah's heart? (Nehemiah 2:12).

And did not the Lord put into King David's heart the vision for rebuilding the temple? (1 Chronicles 22:7).

We could also speak in terms of asking the Holy Spirit to aid us in "visualizing the future." Because of our human frailties, such visualizations must be submitted to members of the leadership team for affirmation. This is not to say that the Holy Spirit's illumination could be flawed. Emphatically not! In every case, the Holy Spirit's illumination is infallible, but our understanding of it could be mistaken.

Application

First, consider how the Holy Spirit uses the Scriptures to bring us to an understanding of the Father's eternal purposes. Each time I approach the Word of God in the Bible, I do so with the full expectation that the Holy Spirit will illuminate my mind with understanding and application. I do not read the Bible simply to become familiar with its content or to score high marks in a Bible knowledge contest. I pore over the Scriptures, meditate on them, study them, and delight in them to bring about transformation of character and alignment with God's will. My time in the Word of God is a response to an inner hunger of heart for spiritual nourishment. It is in the Scriptures that I meet with God for intimate communion every day. The Spirit of truth within me arranges such intimate communion with God.

> My *Resident Rabbi* knows exactly what I need each day.

The Holy Spirit does not teach me all there is in the Bible in one day or in one time of communion with the Father and the Son. I could not possibly handle that much understanding of the Scriptures at one time. Instead of a one-time or even occasional "cloud burst," He graciously gives me "daily showers." My *Resident Rabbi* knows exactly what I need each day; He gives me understanding accordingly. We have said many times that intimacy with God is hunger and thirst driven. My current hunger is much more intense than it was as a church-planting missionary in Malaysia or even in my early days of leadership in the EFCA International Mission. This hunger is stirred in my heart by the Holy Spirit; this appetite is also the wonderful fruit of His work of illumination. There is so much He has to teach me that I have been prompted to double, triple, and quadruple the length of time in the Scriptures. If it were not for both the desire and the delight in the Scriptures, I could not possibly devote so much time to them. I thank my heavenly Father continually for giving me His Holy Spirit to be my *Resident Rabbi.* He is the One who breathes new life into God's Word every morning. He aids me in my quest for intimacy with God.

My personal experience with the Holy Spirit as my Teacher is generally like this. At the most common and frequent level, there are multiple daily promptings, nudgings, impressions, and visualizations. I have come to recognize these as the work of my Divine Instructor, my Tutor who has taken up permanent residence in me. It has been my goal to cultivate immediate recognition of the Holy Spirit's voice through these nudgings and promptings. The mind is a complex creation. It is possible to confuse personal notions with the promptings of the Holy Spirit. We must learn how to distinguish between them and pursue the promptings of the Holy Spirit. All communications from the Holy Spirit must be submitted to the Scriptures or to trusted, godly members of the body, or both. Again, this is not to say that the Holy Spirit's promptings are deficient, but our interpretation of them may well fall short.

> The Holy Spirit sheds light on my path.

A second way the Holy Spirit sheds light on my path is to grant an insight that is life changing and direction setting. It is like a major milestone on the path God has set for me. There have not been many such insights in my years of walking with God, but there have been some, perhaps five or six. They may not seem profound to others, but for me they changed the course of my life. I can humbly share one example. The realization that my highest pursuit as a kingdom leader must be an intimate walk with God changed my outlook, my practices, and my priorities. Intimacy with God has become something of a grid through which I view much of Scripture.

In my experience there has been yet a third way my "Resident Rabbi" works in me. Over the course of fifty-plus years of service in the world of missions, there have been but a few such experiences that shook the very foundations of my being. I have heard others refer to such encounters with God as their Isaiah 6 experience. I see this as accurate, as descriptive of this third way the Holy Spirit has worked in me. Never before was my sin so heinous, never before was the holiness of God so bright and so pure, and never before was the cleansing of God so clean.

I have shared these three levels of the Holy Spirit's work in me with hesitation lest you think that the Holy Spirit will work the same way in your life. He may, but not likely, for He is wonderfully creative in the variety of ways He helps us to understand God's perfect will, and further, to obey it.

It is most humbling to me to realize that the Holy Spirit was the Divine Initiator of every prompting, of every life-changing insight, and of any profound encounter with the Almighty. None originated with me. Such initiations from the Holy Spirit continue today. As noted above, they are the wonderful fruits of the "Resident Rabbi's" work of illumination.

> Our *Resident Rabbi* teaches us what to say in times of sudden, unforeseen crises.

Finally, I share one more context in which our *Resident Rabbi* teaches us. He not only illuminates our minds to comprehend the meaning and application of God's holy Word and communicates with us at varying levels and frequency; He also teaches us what to say in times of sudden, unforeseen crises. Jesus' promise that the Holy Spirit would teach us what to say when hauled before hostile authorities and when threatened with persecution and even death is most comforting and assuring. Speaking to His disciples, Jesus said, *"When you are brought before synagogues, rulers and authorities, do not worry about how you will defend yourselves or what you will say, for* the Holy Spirit will teach you at that time what you should say" (Luke 12:11-12 emphasis added. See also Matthew 10:19-20 and Mark 13:11). Given the level of turmoil in our world, this is a promise every missionary, indeed every child of God, must personally embrace.

So, what does the illuminating/teaching work of the *Resident Rabbi* have to do with intimacy with God? We have said many times that at the heart of intimacy with God is an intense desire for the conscious presence of God. In turn, this desire for God leads to a huge appetite for His Word. These desires are stirred in us by the Holy Spirit, our *Resident Rabbi*. Time in the presence of God and time in the Word of God lead to intimacy with God. There in the presence of God, the Holy Spirit sharpens my spiritual senses to understand and apply the Word of God.

Prayer

Eternal Holy Spirit, I bless You for inspiring the writers of ancient Scripture to record and preserve the very words of God. Thank You for prompting the human authors to write God's words and not their own, to convey God's thoughts and not their own. Because the Scriptures You inspired have in them the very life of the Almighty, they will never diminish in power. Their relevance extends to every generation.

Spirit of truth, what unspeakable joy it is to have You as my Teacher, as the One who quickens my mind to understand and apply the Scriptures, and as the One who empowers me to obey their precepts and embrace their principles. You dwell in me as my Resident Rabbi, as my ever-present Teacher. I delight in

Your uninterrupted readiness to instruct me in the Old and New Testaments. I rejoice that You also dwell in the hearts of all God's children everywhere. You are the Resident Rabbi for all of Jesus' followers in every language and culture.

Gracious Holy Spirit, illuminate my dull, feeble mind to comprehend the Father's eternal purposes. Rein in my wandering thoughts to focus totally on Your truth. Jog my short memory to recall Your unfailing promises. Stir in me a healthy appetite for the living words of God. Let them nourish my soul every day.

Fill my mind with wonder over the perfect connectedness, over the complete harmony there is from book to book and teaching to teaching. Move my mind with a reverent regard for the Holy Bible. These inspired, authoritative words will be my companion for all eternity, for although all of creation will be destroyed, the Scriptures You "breathed" will never pass away.

Whether I read, study, hear, or teach the Scriptures, create in me a humble submission and an immediate obedience to them. This is the longing of my heart, soul, and mind. Amen.

THE HOLY SPIRIT AS MY CONVINCING APOLOGIST

"When the Counselor comes, whom I will send to you from the Father, the Spirit of truth who goes out from the Father, he will testify about me. And you also must testify, for you have been with me from the beginning." (John 15:26-27)

An apologist is one who builds an irrefutable case for the truth. He presents convincing testimony on behalf of the truth. He defends the truth against those who oppose or distort it. He convinces those who waver between truth and error. After the truth has been proclaimed, an apologist defends it with convincing evidence—dismantling all arguments against the truth. Once an apologist has marshaled his incontrovertible evidence for the truth, at least some hearers become converts to the truth.

> The Holy Spirit is in our world to present a witness on behalf of Jesus Christ.

The foregoing describes the wonderful work of the Holy Spirit as our *Convincing Apologist*. He is in our world to present a witness on behalf of Jesus Christ.

In previous essays we have noted that the Holy Spirit serves us as our *Comforting Counselor*, the One who mediates the presence of God to us, and as our *Resident Rabbi*, the One who illuminates our minds to remember, understand, and apply the

Scriptures. In this essay we must take note of yet another one of the divine roles of the Holy Spirit, namely, as the *Convincing Apologist*.

The Holy Spirit has been sent by the Father to testify on behalf of Jesus Christ, the Son. He is in the world to provide a powerful testimony for all that is true about Jesus Christ. He silences those who argue against the truth claims of our Lord. He refutes the errors spread by those opposed to or confused about the gospel of our Lord Jesus. For example, for those who believed that Jesus was merely a carpenter from Nazareth (Matthew 13:55), He counters with convicting arguments for Jesus as the eternal Son of God. For those who claim that Jesus is but one of many ways to God the Father, He testifies to the truth that Jesus is uniquely and exclusively the only way to God.

The Holy Spirit's work as the *Convincing Apologist* is extremely important for the missionary working in Muslim, Hindu, and Buddhist contexts. How will a Muslim who has been told countless times that Jesus is merely one of the many prophets ever be convinced of His deity, His substitutionary death, or His resurrection? How will a Buddhist be willing to discard the idols he has worshipped since childhood to choose Jesus Christ, especially when the Christian faith is viewed as Western? Or how will a Hindu who believes in an endless cycle of reincarnations ever be convinced that there is only one life and after that the judgment before a holy God? Conversion to Christ will take place only as the *Convincing Apologist* constructs a case for the truth.

> Conversion to Christ will take place only as the *Convincing Apologist* constructs a case for the truth.

Jesus' Followers Must Also Be Witnesses

"And you also must testify. . ." (John 15:27). Jesus told His disciples that they too must be His witnesses. The word "must" denotes a sense of

compulsion. Serving as Jesus' witness is not optional for the Christian. Just as the Holy Spirit builds a compelling case for Jesus in this world, the believer must also serve as a convincing apologist for Him. As is often the case in the Scriptures, the human and the divine dimensions are woven together.

The Holy Spirit and all of Jesus' followers are to join together in this task of building an irrefutable case for Jesus Christ. Significantly, this is exactly what the apostles did after the Holy Spirit had been given to them.

We read that *"with great power the apostles continued to testify to the resurrection of the Lord Jesus"* (Acts 4:33). Their goal as witnesses, or as apologists, was to point their hearers to Jesus Christ.

The witness of the Holy Spirit and of the followers of Jesus must not be viewed as separate from each other. Our testimony for Jesus must not be given independently of the Holy Spirit. His witness and ours must be linked together. The Holy Spirit

> The Holy Spirit uses the believer as His vehicle for bold witness for Jesus Christ.

empowers and emboldens Jesus' disciples in their verbal witness for Jesus Christ. Further, the Holy Spirit uses the believer as His vehicle for bold witness for Jesus Christ.

The context of Jesus' teaching on the Holy Spirit as the *Convincing Apologist* is extremely important for our day. We must remember that Jesus' teaching as recorded in John's gospel was given in the Upper Room just hours before His betrayal by Judas and His subsequent substitutionary, sacrificial death for us. Jesus was facing the most critical moments in redemption history. How could He prepare the disciples for the dreadful days ahead? Jesus warned them that the treatment the religious rulers would give Him would also be theirs. They would be hated with the same venomous hatred heaped on Jesus. Little wonder they were filled with anxiety over the future when they heard this. In essence, Jesus forewarned the disciples of dreadful days ahead. They had no confidence that they could stand up to the arguments of the highly educated religious establishment or the might of the Roman authorities. Jesus assured them of the Holy Spirit's convincing case for the truth. They must not be anxious about what they would say when hauled before civil or religious authorities. The Holy Spirit, the *Convincing Apologist,* would provide words that would confound their accusers (Luke 12:11-12).

That Jesus Christ must have a witness in the world is well documented in the gospel of John. For example, John the Baptist, the "voice crying in the wilderness," served as a powerful witness to Jesus (John 5:35); God the Father gave the weightiest of all testimonies to the Son He had sent into our world (5:36); and all of the Scriptures give testimony to Jesus Christ (5:39). We have already noted the witness of the Holy Spirit and of Jesus' followers. This "chorus" of apologetic testimonials for Jesus Christ is both convicting and convincing in our world. It is fitting that Jesus' final words, given to the disciples moments before His ascension to the right hand of the Father, repeated the John 15:27 teaching, namely that they must be His witnesses (Acts 1:8). The disciples were to serve as Jesus' witnesses in the power of the Holy Spirit, never with reliance on their own strength.

Early Church Apologists

Stephen, one of the seven, was a powerfully convincing apologist. He was *"full of faith and of the Holy Spirit"* (Acts 6:5). Those who opposed the truth engaged Stephen in fierce argument, *"but they could not stand up against his wisdom or the Spirit by whom he spoke"* (Acts 6:10). Luke includes Stephen's entire apologetic before the Sanhedrin in Acts 7. Significantly, he devoted more space to Stephen's witness for Jesus Christ than to Peter's Pentecost proclamation or to Paul's message in the synagogue in Pisidian Antioch. Does this make a statement as to the importance of a clear apologetic for Jesus as the Christ?

We can learn from Stephen's apologetic ministry:

- His arguments were empowered by the Holy Spirit.
- His testimony was deeply rooted in Scripture and as a result irrefutable.
- His apologetic was extremely bold in charging the members of the Sanhedrin with the death of Jesus Christ.
- The results of Stephen's witness (testimony, apologetic) were remarkable. He became the first early church martyr through death by stoning. Because of his death, the Christians were scattered widely, spreading the gospel throughout Judea and Samaria. It may also be that Saul of Tarsus, who had heard Stephen's compelling arguments for Jesus as the Messiah and who witnessed Stephen's stoning and consented to his death, began to have doubts about his crusade against Jesus Christ.

Apollos was also a powerful apologist. He was a *"learned man with a thorough knowledge of the Scriptures"* (Acts 18:24). Apollos' apologetic ministry in Achaia is described by Luke in these words: *"He vigorously refuted the Jews in public debate, proving from the Scriptures that Jesus was the Christ"* (Acts 18:28). That is the work of an apologist. We can also learn from Apollos' apologetic ministry:

- Apollos had a strong grasp of the Scriptures.
- Apollos was able to withstand and even overcome the objections of the Jews.
- Apollos was able to present proof that Jesus was the Christ.

There are common characteristics in these two New Testament apologists. Both were strong in the Scriptures. Both demonstrated boldness in presenting their arguments; they seemed absolutely fearless. In both cases there were remarkable results in the form of fruitful evangelism among the hearers.

Much of the apostle Paul's preaching ministry was apologetic in nature. Note especially Luke's description of Paul's apologetic ministry at Corinth: *"Every Sabbath he reasoned in the synagogue,* trying to persuade Jews and Greeks" (Acts 18:4, emphasis added). Persuasion toward conversion is precisely the work of an apologist.

The clearest statement on the apostles' witness for Jesus Christ may well be the words of Peter at Cornelius' house in Caesarea. Peter said, *"We are* witnesses *of everything he did in the country of the Jews and in Jerusalem. They killed him by hanging Him on a tree, but God raised him from the dead on the third day and caused him to be seen. He was not seen by all of the people, but by* witnesses *whom God had already chosen—by us who ate and drank with Him after He rose from the dead"* (Acts 10:39-41, emphasis added). Peter's witness for the truth about Jesus was accompanied by a miraculous outpouring of the Holy Spirit on Cornelius' Gentile household.

Application

Why did Jesus charge His disciples to be His witnesses? What qualified them to be His witnesses in the world? Once again we encounter the "with Him" principle. Three years earlier, Jesus' primary reason for choosing His followers had been that they spend time together. He had much to teach them about their mission in the future. When He first called them, He did not immediately unveil the Great Commission. Only after being with His disciples in every conceivable life situation did Jesus commission them to be His witnesses (Acts 1:8). Jesus' relationship with the Twelve began with an invitation to be with Him to be discipled and ended with the commission to testify for Him throughout the world.

If we have doubt about building a case for Jesus as Lord together with the Holy Spirit, please note again Jesus' words. He promised the disciples that the Holy Spirit would serve as the *Convincing Apologist*. *"You* also *must testify,"* (John 15:27, emphasis added) Jesus said to His followers. The word *also* makes clear that we join the Holy Spirit in our witness for Jesus.

> We too must spend time with Jesus before going out to be witnesses for Jesus.

The lesson for us today is that we too must spend time with Jesus before going out to be witnesses for Jesus. The order is intimacy with God before service for God, knowing and loving God before serving God. The disciples had the unique privilege of being eyewitnesses of Jesus' life and ministry for three full years. Their association with Jesus dated back to the very beginning of His public ministry. The invitation to be with Jesus is extended to us today as surely as it was to Jesus' apostles. Our task of testifying for Jesus must be the overflow of a life lived in intimate relationship with Jesus.

Prayer

Gracious Holy Spirit, I rejoice in Your witness to my Lord and Savior, Jesus Christ. You are the Convincing Apologist, the One who builds a compelling case for Jesus Christ as the eternal Son of God. You gently convince hearers of the truth as it is in Jesus. You refute all arguments against Jesus as the only way to the Father. You defend the truths about Jesus as recorded in the Holy Bible. Convincing Apologist, I rest securely in Your Christ-centered witness. You will never lead anyone away from Jesus, only closer to Him. Only with Your help, gracious Spirit of truth, can we call Jesus "Lord."

I am moved by the complete harmony there is in the Trinity where Father, Son, and Holy Spirit are co-equal and none is greater than the other. I rejoice in the Holy Spirit's mission to bear witness to the Son and to give glory to His Name. I realize, dear Holy Spirit, that You will never miss one opportunity to bear witness to the eternal Son of God.

Your assignment to us is to bear witness to Jesus in our Jerusalem, Judea, Samaria, and the uttermost parts of the world. How wonderful that You empower us to bear this global witness to the Son, to honor His name, to build an irrefutable case for His deity and lordship, and to turn men to trust in His atoning work on the cross.

I rejoice that Your convincing apologetic for Jesus is penetrating deeper and deeper into Muslim, Hindu, and Buddhist countries. I long for that certain day when followers of all religions, philosophies, and ideologies will bow the knee to Jesus Christ and confess Him as their Lord. Your witness to Jesus, dear Holy Spirit, is always clear, appropriate, and compelling. Help me to bear such a witness for Jesus, my Master, too.

This is the prayer You have helped me offer up to the Father. Amen.

THE HOLY SPIRIT AS MY CONVICTING EVANGELIST

"But I tell you the truth: It is for your good that I am going away. *Unless I go away, the Counselor will not come to you; but if I go, I will send him to you.* When he comes, he will convict the world of guilt in regard to sin and righteousness and judgment: *in regard to sin, because men do not believe in me; in regard to righteousness, because I am going to the Father, where you can see me no longer; and in regard to judgment, because the prince of this world now stands condemned."* (John 16:7-11, emphasis added)

As our *Comforting Counselor*, the Holy Spirit makes possible an intimate walk with the Father. As our *Resident Rabbi*, He helps us to understand, apply, and obey the Scriptures. And as our *Convincing Apologist*, He builds a case for the truth as it is in Jesus Christ, the eternal Son of God.

In the text forming the foundation for this essay, the Holy Spirit fills the role as our *Convicting Evangelist.* Evangelism is His primary role in the world of lost people. Most of the work done by the Holy Spirit is either in the believer or in the church, the body of believers. Here, however, Jesus makes very clear that the Holy Spirit's evangelistic role is also in the world where lost people reside. So then, the Holy Spirit's three spheres of activity are in every believer everywhere, in the global Christian church, and in God's world at large. We must not forget that whether in the believer individually, in the church collectively, or in the world globally, the work of the Holy Spirit is always Christocentric; that is, its focus is always on Jesus Christ and not on Himself.

Jesus made clear that the Holy Spirit would not come if He did not return to the Father. In fact, Jesus said clearly that His return to the right hand of the Father was for their good. How so? The spread of the gospel would have been geographically limited had Jesus remained with the disciples. Comparatively few would hear the gospel if its spread depended on Jesus' bodily presence and His audible voice. Jesus' final command to all of His followers was to be His witnesses in Jerusalem, Judea, Samaria, and in the farthest parts of the world (see Acts 1:8). Obedience to the Great Commission would have been an utter impossibility apart from the Holy Spirit's simultaneous control in all believers everywhere.

> Jesus' final command to all of His followers was to be His witnesses.

So, the advantage to Jesus' return to the right hand of the Father was that through the Holy Spirit, His work of evangelism would be worldwide. Jesus' personal mission on earth had been to seek and to save the lost (see Luke 19:10). Bringing the lost to Jesus through His devoted followers would also be the work of the Holy Spirit in the world. The big difference would be that whereas Jesus' proclamation of the gospel was limited to one place at one time, the Holy Spirit would be the *Omnipresent Evangelist*. Let all twenty-first-century missionaries take note: Only through the direction and power of the Holy Spirit can the work of evangelism be international in nature.

The Holy Spirit Convicts of Sin

Precisely what did Jesus mean when He told His disciples that the Holy Spirit would convict of sin? Picture a courtroom scene in which the

Holy Spirit hands down a guilty verdict to all lost sinners. He confronts and condemns lost men and women in their sin. When He defines sin, the *Convicting Evangelist* does so from the perspective of the Father's absolute holiness. The Holy Spirit's guilty verdict is of sin so serious that it causes all men and women to fall far short of God's standard of holiness. This sin is doing what should not be done and neglecting to do what should be done. When the guilty sinner hears the Holy Spirit's sentence, his tongue is silenced. He has no words of argument or objection to offer. His conviction is irresistible and final. The sinner cannot but agree with the Holy Spirit's verdict. There is no further appeal. The Holy Spirit guides the lost person in a sincere, heartfelt utterance of the sinner's prayer: *"God, have mercy on me, a sinner"* (Luke 18:13). With anguish of soul and deep repentance, the convicted sinner cries to God for mercy, and praise be to God, he receives it!

It is not natural for a lost person to admit to being a sinner and in need of a Savior, but this is precisely what the Holy Spirit helps him to do. The *Convicting Evangelist* brings the proud, arrogant person to stand before our holy God with head bowed in silent shame and with heart pleading for mercy, and praise be to God, he receives it!

It is my conviction that all followers of Jesus Christ must be evangelists. Paul exhorted timid Timothy to do the work of an evangelist (2 Timothy 4:5). The Holy Spirit takes our feeble, disorganized words and through them convicts the hearers of sin. Unless the Holy Spirit adds His convicting power to our words of witness, they will all

> Unless the Holy Spirit adds His convicting power to our words of witness, they will all fall to the ground.

fall to the ground. It is utterly impossible for us to generate repentance in the heart of a lost person. This is the unique work of the *Convicting Evangelist.* How misguided a notion it is to think that we could do evangelism without the *Convicting Evangelist* working in us, with us, and through us.

The sin the Holy Spirit most often convicts lost people of is their failure to trust in Jesus alone for their salvation. Jesus Christ is uniquely and exclusively the only Savior for all men; apart from Him there is no salvation. Only He can give the gift of eternal life. Only He can forgive sin. Only Jesus Christ can inscribe our names in the Lamb's Book of Life. The Holy Spirit will not allow such common watered-down notions about Jesus Christ as follows: That He was merely a good teacher; He was but the son of a carpenter who lived in Nazareth; He was a man who lived a good life worthy of our emulation; or that He was one of the ancient prophets. Nothing less than an unqualified, clear confession that Jesus is the Christ, the eternal Son of the living God, will suffice for our *Convicting Evangelist.*

The Holy Spirit Convicts of Righteousness

Another facet of the Holy Spirit's work in the world as the *Convicting Evangelist* is to bring the lost to rely on Jesus' righteousness and not on their own failed, feeble attempts to be good. Salvation through good works is a deeply entrenched global heresy. Only the *Convicting Evangelist* can root it out. Though he does not know it with certainty, man's inclination is to think that personal efforts will ultimately suffice to satisfy a holy God, especially if he is sincere. If only his good deeds outweigh the bad, he thinks that he will be acceptable to a loving God. Not so! The *Convicting Evangelist* contrasts the absolute standard of God's holy character with our own good deeds by depicting them as filthy rags: *"all our righteous acts are like filthy rags . . ."* (Isaiah 64:6). That lost man is incapable of contributing anything to his salvation is a bitter pill to swallow. Such a confession is a crushing blow to his pride. He stubbornly clings to the false teaching that at the very least God will combine his goodness with the saving work of Jesus.

As He convicts the lost person of the futility of relying on his own goodness to be saved, the Holy Spirit says to him, "Cease striving to satisfy a holy God with your personal goodness. Look to Jesus Christ, the spotless Lamb of God to be saved. Trust in Him alone for your salvation. Jesus' substitutionary death on the cross for you is the only sacrifice for sin I will accept."

The Holy Spirit Convicts of Judgment

When the followers of Jesus talk about a judgment to come, the lost laugh. They laughed hilariously in Noah's day, but precisely in God's time, judgment did come in the form of a global flood. In Lot's time, only he and his two daughters escaped judgment. Everyone else treated the judgment by fire and brimstone lightly or as a sick joke. The *Convicting Evangelist* makes clear that final and eternal judgment of the lost is as

> The Holy Spirit confronts the lost with a judgment to come.

certain as the judgment faced by Satan, that proud and rebellious angel of light. When the Holy Spirit convicts of judgment, the lost tremble with fear. This does not mean that they will all bow the knee in submission to Jesus Christ. It does mean, however, that when the Holy Spirit confronts the lost with a judgment to come, they know in their heart of hearts that this is the truth. If they were willing to admit the state of their heart upon hearing such foreboding news, it would be one of terror. Such is the work of the *Convicting Evangelist* when He hands those who reject Jesus Christ over to the Father for judgment. The message of Jesus' followers is that Jesus is Lord and that Satan has been judged already. All who refuse to believe in Him will suffer Satan's fate.

In summary, apart from the Holy Spirit's partnership in the work of evangelism, we could spend a lifetime circling the globe earning millions of frequent flyer miles and working our "fingers to the bone" without gaining one single convert. Jesus made clear to His followers both then and now that we are to be His witnesses everywhere, but also that this is an impossible assignment apart from the accompanying, convicting power of the Holy Spirit. Jesus never intended for us to launch evangelistic thrusts into the world of lost people in our own strength through our own programs. Instead, He promised to send the Holy Spirit to work with us and in us as the *Convicting Evangelist*.

Once again we must ask the question, "What does doing evangelism in the power and under the direction of the *Convicting Evangelist* have to do with intimacy with God?" After all, intimacy with God is the theme of this series of essays. We have said repeatedly that one of the principle tasks of the Holy Spirit is to mediate the presence of God to the believer. I can say from painful experience that doing evangelism is a difficult assignment and a dutiful task when Jesus Christ is distant, but when I desire God and delight in Him, evangelism is both enjoyable and fruitful. The lost are attracted to someone who lives his or her life in the conscious presence of God. Before spending time with the lost publicly to introduce them to the Savior, we must devote significant time to enjoying the presence of God privately. Here is a wonderful truth: The Holy Spirit mediates the presence of God to us and in the process empowers and guides us into a life of spontaneous evangelism.

My personal commitment to the Lord Jesus is to take advantage of every witnessing opportunity orchestrated by the Spirit of God. The Holy Spirit's heart yearns for lost people and has on numerous occasions taken me up on that commitment. Here are a few illustrations of the *Convicting Evangelist* clearly arranging witnessing experiences.

My first such experience came at the age of sixteen on a train in Alberta between Edmonton and Peace River. The Spirit of God nudged me to give a gospel tract to the man across the aisle from me. After much hesitation, I obeyed. This man had been prepared by the Holy Spirit. I watched as he carefully read the tract. When he was done, I got up and sat down beside him. After I explained the meaning of the gospel in the tract, he bowed his head with me and prayed to receive Christ. This was the first time in my life I experienced the joy of leading someone to trust in Jesus alone for his salvation.

Another time I was passing an old, rundown house in downtown Minneapolis. An older man sitting all alone in his chair on the veranda caught my attention. The Holy Spirit clearly nudged me to change my walking direction to talk with this total stranger. Obediently I did so. Very quickly I realized that my dear *Convicting Evangelist* had gone before me to prepare this man to trust in Jesus alone for his salvation. What unspeakable joy filled my heart as I went on my way.

There have been many opportunities to witness for Christ on flights. On one such occasion, I prayed fervently during my early morning time of communion with the Father, "O, Lord, today, let me be Your evangelist." I had never prayed exactly like this before, but this brief prayer has become a frequent plea to God. Checking in for my flight to Miami, I discovered that I had been upgraded to first class. A businessman asked if I would trade seats so he could sit with a friend. I willingly moved across the aisle. My seatmate, a nurse, had never flown first class before. Furthermore, we discovered that the seat she had taken beside me belonged to someone else; he graciously allowed her to stay where she was. By this time I knew that the Holy Spirit was orchestrating a witnessing opportunity. It did not take a lot of further prayer to determine whether I should witness to this lady. Before we touched down in Miami three hours later, God had answered my

> Doing the work of evangelism and intimacy with God are inseparably linked together.

prayer and graciously used me to be His evangelist. My seatmate prayed with me to trust in Jesus alone for her salvation. What unspeakable joy flooded my soul over another sinner who had repented and believed.

So you see dear brothers and sisters, doing the work of evangelism and intimacy with God are inseparably linked together. Faithfulness and fruitfulness in evangelism flows naturally and spontaneously out of an intimate walk with God.

Prayer

Dear Holy Spirit, the Father sent You into our world to be the Convicting Evangelist. As the Convicting Evangelist You yearn for lost people everywhere. You draw them to the feet of Jesus, the Savior of the world. You open their heart's door for the Lord Jesus to enter.

You stir in us a compassion for the straying, shepherdless sheep. You irrigate our arid hearts with the same love the waiting Father has for His prodigal sons and daughters. You prompt us to share the gospel with those whose hearts You have prepared to receive the truth.

Spirit of truth, You are in us and around us to do the work of evangelism. Your work as Convicting Evangelist knows no barriers. There is no country, parliament, city, hamlet, or even household where You do not strive with the lost to bow the knee to Jesus Christ. Neither is there a culture, language, or religion where You do not do Your work as our Convicting Evangelist.

All-knowing Spirit, You were also sent by the Father to be His Condemning Prosecutor. You have handed down a guilty verdict against all who willfully refuse to believe in Jesus, against all who rely on their own good deeds to save them, and against all who will share in Satan's final judgment.

When we open our mouths to proclaim the life-transforming gospel, You give us suitable, sensitive words. You flood our souls with unspeakable joy as we share the gospel. You replace our timidity and fear with boldness. You give us favor in the eyes of lost people. As we witness for Jesus, You whisper into the ear of the unbeliever, "This is the truth! Receive it!" You bestow the priceless gifts of faith and repentance on the hearers.

Dear Holy Spirit, I love You as my Compassionate Companion in the work of evangelism. I renew my commitment to take advantage of every witnessing opportunity You orchestrate. As You directed Philip to speak to the Ethiopian, and Peter to Cornelius the Centurion, so lead me to lost people whose hearts You are opening to receive the truth. To make good this resolve, I need Your direction and Your power. This is my fervent prayer to You, Sovereign Spirit of the Lord. Amen.

THE HOLY SPIRIT AS MY SUPERINTENDING GUIDE
PART 1

"Paul and his companions traveled throughout the region of Phrygia and Galatia, having been kept by the Holy Spirit from preaching the word in the province of Asia. *When they came to the border of Mysia, they tried to enter Bithynia,* but the Spirit of Jesus would not allow them to. *So they passed by Mysia and went down to Troas. During the night Paul had a vision of a man of Macedonia standing and begging him, 'Come over to Macedonia and help us.' After Paul had seen the vision, we got ready at once to leave for Macedonia, concluding that* God had called us *to preach the gospel to them."* (Acts 16:6-10, emphasis added)

In the Old Testament, the Israelites' movements were guided by a cloud during the day and a pillar of fire by night (see Exodus 40:36-38). God provided guidance 24–7. The good news is that He still does. Whenever the cloud lifted from over the Tent of Meeting, everyone knew that they must break camp in preparation to move on. Because the cloud represented both the presence and glory of God, the signal to move on or to stop came from God Himself. What the Israelites experienced each time they stopped or continued their journey to the Promised Land was divine guidance. The good news is that we too can experience divine guidance in the twenty-first century.

Interestingly, God's cloud and fire guidance for Israel was not given to an individual, not even to Moses, but to everyone in the Israelite camp. God chose to reveal His plan to the entire Israelite community. The divine principle of corporate guidance continues today. We must beware of claims to private, individualistic insights into the will of God. Whenever the Holy Spirit chooses to give guidance to an individual, it usually awaits the affirmation of others, in most cases a local church leadership team.

The means God chooses to guide us today are different from the wilderness pillar of fire and cloud, but His direction for us today is no less divine, no less certain, and I should add, no less clear. The surest thing about the will of God is that there can be certainty about knowing and doing the will of God.

The Holy Spirit is wonderfully creative in His choice of means to guide us. Over the centuries, however, His most common way of guiding us has been through the Scriptures He inspired human authors to write. The surest way to discern the will of God is to invest daily time studying the Word of God. Being familiar with the Word of God leads to a clear understanding of the will of God. We cannot go astray from the perfect will of God as long as we are obedient to the inspired Word of God.

> The surest way to discern the will of God is to invest daily time studying the Word of God.

At times we must be willing to devote additional blocks of time to poring over the Scriptures. When we do so, the Holy Spirit helps us to think God's very thoughts. As we meditate on His Word, we can fully expect to hear Him speak words of guidance into our situations. This is because the same Holy Spirit who inspired the Scriptures will also tutor us in their understanding and application. Sometimes the Holy Spirit uses more dramatic means such as a vision or even a voice to give us direction, but these must not be viewed as the norm for receiving guidance.

In this essay on intimacy with God and the Holy Spirit, we will view the Holy Spirit as our *Superintending Guide.* Reading through the Book of Acts, we cannot miss the *Superintending Guide's* role of energizing, directing, orchestrating, and supervising the spread of the gospel and the planting of the church. There is no dispute over the fact that He is the power behind the birth, growth, and expansion of the early church.

The remarkable account (Acts 16:6-10) of the Holy Spirit's clear direction for Paul and His itinerant gospel preaching team has some important lessons about guidance to teach us. Paul's plan was to go to Asia, but his *Superintending Guide* blocked the way, not only once but twice. We tend to think of receiving divine guidance as those times when the Holy Spirit tells us where to go and what to do, like the time He directed the church at Antioch to launch the mission to the Gentiles. In the Acts 16 account, however, the Holy Spirit restrains twice in succession and constrains once. Saying no to us is as valid guidance as when He says yes. The *Superintending Guide's* restraints and constraints convey identical messages; He will never send us mixed signals. Although the *Superintending Guide* employs a range of means to communicate His guidance to us, we can fully expect total alignment in all of them.

In Acts 16 we see the Holy Spirit redirecting Paul and his team. Paul had what he thought was clear direction for his team. There is no indication that Paul exercised surprise over this redirection. They found themselves in Phrygia and Galatia because the Holy Spirit had nudged them away from Asia. In the course of their travels, they wanted to enter the province of Bithynia, but again they were not allowed to proceed. Twice in a row, the Holy Spirit prevented them from going where they thought they should go. In addition to these two successive closed doors, Paul was given a vision in which he was summoned to go to Macedonia. What was going on? We now know that the Spirit of God was directing Paul and his team Europe-ward. We now look back on the *Superintending Guide's* direction as a major turning point in the history of the global missionary enterprise. The Pauline team could not have known how far-reaching this new direction from their *Superintending Guide* was. Theirs was not to ask why but simply to obey the leading of the Holy Spirit.

What specific lessons can we learn from Paul's dramatic encounter with the Holy Spirit as his *Superintending Guide*?

The *Superintending Guide* Has the Big Picture

Whereas Paul and his team could see a detail or two on their human "radar screen," the *Superintending Guide* had in mind the sovereign Lord's comprehensive plan. When it comes to guidance for our missionary endeavors, our limitations add up to a severe handicap. Even tomorrow is unclear to us, let alone next year or an entire lifetime. We need the Holy Spirit to reveal His overall plan, or the long view of missions. Paul could not possibly have known that the Holy Spirit was changing his course so that all of Europe, and eventually the entire Western world, could be evangelized. We in the West are the beneficiaries of the Holy Spirit's guidance and the Pauline team's obedience. Our task in the twenty-first century is to respond obediently to His direction so that our generation too can hear the gospel.

The *Superintending Guide* Opens and Closes Doors

The Holy Spirit said no to Asia as well as to Bithynia. In both of these instances Paul and his team accepted a closed door as from the Holy Spirit. The entire team viewed the vision of the man from Macedonia begging for help as an open door. We do not know the exact means the Holy Spirit used to guide Paul and His team. Luke does not include them lest we try to imitate them in the twenty-first century. Did the Holy Spirit speak audibly? Did He unify the team around a strong conviction?

> We never need to flounder about in uncertainty.

Was it a conversation about the needs in Macedonia with Dr. Luke who joined the team at this time? (Note the first of the so-called "we passages," Acts 16:10ff.) Whatever the method used by the *Superintending Guide*, Paul and his team understood what they were to do. Understanding and obeying the will of God is the goal of the *Superintending Guide's* guidance. We never need to flounder about in uncertainty.

The entire team was united in its conclusion that God was calling them westward to Macedonia. This mix of means required sensitivity to the voice of the Holy Spirit. It is important to note that two successive closed doors did not lead the Pauline team to conclude that God had withdrawn His call or even that they should put the Mission to the Gentiles on hold for a time. Closed doors should neither puzzle nor frustrate us; they are a valid means used by the *Superintending Guide* to direct our steps.

The *Superintending Guide* Takes the Lead in Providing Direction

Clearly, the *Superintending Guide* took the lead in providing counsel for the Pauline team. As Jesus had promised, the Holy Spirit would take His place as His followers' Counselor. The Counselor is identified successively as the "Holy Spirit" (Acts 16:6), as the "Spirit of Jesus" (Acts 16:7), and as "God" (Acts 16:10). The implication is clear. All three members of the Trinity, i.e., the Father, Son, and Holy Spirit, are engaged in providing guidance, but it is the *Superintending Guide* who takes the lead and is actually mentioned first in this case. Guiding the global missionary movement is one of His specialties.

Personal Experience with My *Superintending Guide*

Allow me to share a small part my own experience with the Holy Spirit over more than five decades of walking with God. I have come to recognize three categories of His working in me.

First, there are the unmistakable daily promptings and nudgings from the Holy Spirit. They can also be identified as clear inner convictions, as strong impressions, or as an inner sense that this is what I must do. Such inner convictions are not to be confused with intuition or the so-called sixth sense. They originate with the Holy Spirit as He fills or controls us.

Second, far less frequent than the nudges and prompts, is what I call direction-setting ministry changes in the form of fresh vision written on our hearts by the Spirit of God—new initiatives, major shifts in missiological thinking, the reconfiguration of a leadership team, etc.

Third, even less frequent are those rare occasions when the Holy Spirit worked a life-transforming work in me. Years later, these transformations are as vivid as though they happened this morning. I can recall only three such encounters with my *Superintending Guide.*

It is important to note that the Holy Spirit is the great Initiator of all that happens in each of these three categories. We cannot credit our own spiritual depth, our mental brilliance, or our keen insights. At most, we were the human instruments to and through whom the Holy Spirit communicated His will.

Identifying these three categories has been very helpful to me. I must, however, exercise care to avoid thinking that the Holy Spirit is limited to deal with me in these three categories. He is not. As noted above, the Holy Spirit is wonderfully creative in the way He works in us. It should not surprise us that He "tailors" His approach uniquely to each Christian, leadership team, local church, and to each movement of churches.

Daily Nudgings and Promptings

This category of the Holy Spirit's work in us could be characterized as living all of life under the conscious, continuous, complete control of the Holy Spirit. Paul describes it as living according to the Spirit, controlled by the Spirit, and led by the Spirit (see Romans 8). I understand, by the way,

> We must cultivate sensitivity to the voice of the Holy Spirit.

that the *control* of the Holy Spirit and the *fullness* of the Holy Spirit are synonymous. To respond promptly to the daily nudges and prompts, we must cultivate sensitivity to the voice of the Holy Spirit.

The *Superintending Guide's* nudge or prompt may be to engage in spontaneous intercession, to speak a word of encouragement, to share a verbal witness, to ask forgiveness for an inappropriate comment or attitude, an insight to be woven into a message or a writing project, or a new idea to share with fellow workers. There is great joy reserved for the believer who goes through each day allowing the Holy Spirit to orchestrate conversations, thoughts, e-mail communications, etc. At the end of each day, it is most gratifying to look back over a day that pleased God and fulfilled His purposes. My sense is that the cultivation of sensitivities to the nudgings and promptings of the Holy Spirit trains our ears to hear His voice in the larger, less frequent happenings.

Direction-Setting Insights that Lead to Major Ministry Change

Less frequent are the direction-setting insights into God's purposes— major shifts in strategy, the adoption of new initiatives, significant changes in structure, the creation of new leadership positions, etc. I define this category as the Holy Spirit's work of bringing about the convergence of vision, ideas, information about great needs, provision of money and personnel for implementation, and consensus among those responsible to hear the voice of our *Superintending Guide*. We desperately need the Holy Spirit's counsel for such weighty matters.

By way of illustration, I listed twenty-two such items in my final report to the board of our mission, a report that spanned twelve years. There is great joy in recognizing the power and counsel of our *Superintending Guide* at work in our lives and ministry.

Life-Transforming Encounters

Over the course of almost five decades of ministry, apart from my conversion and call to a life of involvement in global missionary endeavors, I can think of only three experiences with the Holy Spirit that rose to the level of a life-transforming encounter. You may not consider them to be dramatic, but they radically changed the course of my life.

First, in my senior year of Bible College in 1957 at the age of twenty-two, I discovered a major blind spot in my vision for missionary work. I had not understood the centrality of the local church in the global missionary enterprise. My view of missions was almost totally parachurch. I came to realize that it was the church that commissioned missionaries, and furthermore, it was to the church that the sovereign Lord of the Harvest had assigned the task of completing the Great Commission. This encounter under the Holy Spirit's tutelage forever changed my understanding of God's plan to place the church into the heart of an Acts 1:8 vision for the world.

My second life-transforming encounter with my *Superintending Guide* took place near the end of 1964 at the age of thirty during a personal day of private prayer and fasting. I saw clearly that I could never hope to plant the church without the fullness of the Holy Spirit.

Third, in December of 1996 in Moscow, I was awakened twice in the middle of the night with an overwhelming desire for an intimate walk with God, a hunger that has persisted and grown in intensity over these fifteen years.

In all three instances, the Holy Spirit was the gracious Initiator. By this I mean that I had nothing whatsoever to do with these encounters except to respond to them with grateful, humble obedience. I did not plan for them or anticipate them. I do not know if there are other such encounters that await me. Since the initiative for each of these life-transforming encounters comes from the Holy Spirit, He must be given all of the glory.

Application

Discerning the will of God is not a mysterious matter or a difficult riddle to be solved. Our heavenly Father wants us to be fully aware of His plans for us. So that we might know His plans, He has given us the Holy Spirit to superintend and empower our personal lives and our ministries. One of the prayers the Holy Spirit has written on my heart has literally become a daily petition to my Father: *Dear Father, I pray that throughout this day I shall know the conscious, complete, and continuous control of my Superintending Guide over my thoughts, motivations, attitudes, and conversations.* The daily answers to that prayer have contributed immeasurably to going progressively deeper in knowing, loving, and serving God; in short, to a more intimate walk with God.

THE HOLY SPIRIT AS MY SUPERINTENDING GUIDE PART 2

The Book of Acts is an account of the post-ascension ministry of Jesus' disciples. For this reason the name commonly given to this book is the Acts of the Apostles. A closer look leads us to the inevitable conclusion that this is also, and perhaps more accurately, an account of the Acts of the Holy Spirit. Luke's account portrays the Holy Spirit as the Superintendent of all that happened in this thirty-year history of the early church.

The Book of Acts begins, continues, and ends with the superintending, empowering, controlling, guiding, convicting, and choosing work of the Holy Spirit. There is no question but that the Holy Spirit is in charge of the first Church Planting Movement (CPM).

Before Creation, the Holy Spirit hovered over the empty darkness to bring order out of chaos. Now, we see Him giving shape and direction to this new emerging church. He is the divine dynamic behind every word of witness uttered, every message preached, each transformed life, every intercessory prayer, and the early church's numerical growth and geographic expansion.

Jesus commanded the apostles to wait (Acts 1:4) for the outpouring of the Holy Spirit before attempting obedience to the Great Commission.

Apart from the energizing power of the Holy Spirit, the apostles' assignment to launch a CPM would fail miserably.

Our tendency is to wait too little and to charge ahead too quickly with programs. That the disciples would receive power when the Holy Spirit came upon them and that they would be effective witnesses for Jesus were two inevitabilities. Jesus had promised, *"You* will *receive power,"* and *"you* will *be my witnesses."* The question was simply: would they be obedient to Jesus' command to wait for the gift of the Holy Spirit from the Father? (Acts 1:4-8, emphasis added).

To give us a sense of the pervasiveness of the Holy Spirit's presence in the Book of Acts, please note the following list of His activities in the launching of the first CPM. I do not suggest that the Holy Spirit will do His work the same today as in Acts. He will not. He is wonderfully creative in His choice of methods to do His work. Our focus today must not be on how He did His work in the first CPM, but that He did in fact work powerfully. We must expect that the Holy Spirit will be as prominently active today as He was during the birth of the early church, albeit in different ways.

> We must expect that the Holy Spirit will be as prominently active today.

Empowered to Serve

The Holy Spirit was to be the apostles' sole source of spiritual power for launching a CPM (Acts 1:8, cf. 4:33). It was that simple! There would be no other dynamic, no other energy for their mission. Reliance on organization, programs, budgets, professionalism, or even human charisma would doom the mission to failure. There would be but one source of spiritual power.

Two thousand years later, this has not changed. The list of competing alternatives for the power of the Holy Spirit is longer today than ever, but the peril of relying on them is as disastrous now as it would have been for the first CPM leaders. Who among us has not longed for greater spiritual power in our service for God? The Holy Spirit is willing to energize the child of God with the same power so visible in the Acts of the Apostles.

Emboldened to Proclaim

The Holy Spirit gave the movement leaders unusual boldness in a variety of contexts (Acts 4:8, 31; 7:51-52; 13:9), boldness that silenced and amazed even their enemies. One of the most remarkable post-Pentecost changes in all of the apostles, especially noticeable in Peter, was their new boldness. His former brashness was replaced with uncompromising boldness. Just over a month earlier, Peter had denied Jesus three times. After the power of the Holy Spirit filled him, Peter's cowering timidity gave way to fearless, public identification with Jesus and His message. Reading the accounts of the movement leaders' "in your face" boldness before religious and civil leaders all but takes one's breath away.

Who among us has not longed for greater boldness in our witness for Jesus Christ? The same Holy Spirit who helped Peter and others to speak the Word of God with boldness will also embolden us. The apostles and others asked for boldness; the Holy Spirit gave it to them (Acts 4:29, 31).

Powerfully Persuasive Teaching

Stephen's antagonists could not withstand his convicting words (Acts 6:10). They had two alternatives—either bow the knee to Christ or violently oppose Stephen. They chose the latter and stoned him to death. That the Holy Spirit spoke powerful words of conviction through the early church movement leaders was their common experience. The Holy Spirit took the messages preached by Peter, Paul, Philip, Stephen, and others and drove them like arrows into the hearts of the hearers. The Holy Spirit breathed life into words that would ordinarily neither convict nor persuade.

Endowed with Discernment

The Holy Spirit gave discernment to Peter to detect Ananias and Sapphira's conspiracy to lie to God and to His church (Acts 5:3, 9). Peter did not call upon some secret, inner, psychic powers to tip him off to their duplicity. Guided by the Holy Spirit, Peter sensed that Ananias and Sapphira were lying. This was more than a hunch, a sixth sense, or a premonition; it was Holy Spirit-given discernment. This gift of discernment is as important in today's twenty-first century church as it was for Peter in the mother church in Jerusalem.

Interestingly, the Acts account does not record another such event. There was only one. The lesson was clear. The Holy Spirit would not tolerate deceit and hypocrisy in the church. The Holy Spirit gave Peter the discernment to detect what was false. He gives a similar gift to the body of Christ to detect teaching out of alignment with the Scriptures.

Spirit-Filled Administrators

The fullness of the Holy Spirit was to be a qualification for service, including the administrative tasks in the church (Acts 6:4, 5). The Holy Spirit's power and control was not limited to those with the public speaking and leading gifts. He must control the administrative tasks as well. He must empower the administrators as well as the ministers. As the CPM grew and gained momentum, new and different structures became necessary. The Holy Spirit guided the church to structures that were uniquely suited to its growth and to its multi-cultural context, including Jewish and Greek people.

Structures in the twenty-first-century church are not the same as in the twenty-first-century corporate world. Organization in the Jerusalem congregation as well as in today's church must be the product of the Holy Spirit's work. The apostles made the intentional choice to "give [their] attention to prayer and the ministry of the Word" (Acts 6:4). Ministry was to remain their priority. Administrative tasks were to be shouldered by other Spirit-filled workers in the church.

Joy in Persecution

The Holy Spirit's fullness was (is) synonymous with complete joy (Acts 13:49-52). The Spirit of God bears the fruit of joy in and through us. The context of the Spirit's supernatural joy on this occasion was persecution. It is never natural for the followers of Jesus to be filled with joy in the midst of opposition. Apart from the fullness of the Holy Spirit, it is impossible to exhibit genuine joy. Joy in the midst of adverse circumstances is a powerfully attractive spiritual grace in a world where a happy state is totally dependent on good circumstances.

> Apart from the fullness of the Holy Spirit, it is impossible to exhibit genuine joy.

Comfort in Persecution

The Holy Spirit encouraged a church that had just come through terrible persecution led by Saul of Tarsus (Acts 9:31). We must not forget that the Holy Spirit is the *Paraclete*, the one who comes alongside us to administer comfort. He comforts the individual believer as well as the church. Jesus had promised that He would not abandon His followers; they would not become orphans after His ascension. The Holy Spirit would be in Jesus' followers speaking words of comfort and encouragement. The persecution unleashed by the martyrdom of Stephen could have discouraged the Christians and forced them to retreat into hiding, but the opposite happened. In spite of the fierce persecution, the church grew both numerically and geographically. The Holy Spirit orchestrated a time of fierce persecution followed by a time of calm and comfort.

Superintending Guide

The Holy Spirit provided direction for Philip to witness to the Ethiopian eunuch (Acts 8:29), for Peter to go to Cornelius' house (Acts 10:19; 11:12), for Paul and his team (Acts 16:6-10) to go to Europe instead of continuing on their Asia-ward course, as well as for Paul personally on his way to Jerusalem (Acts 20:22). Each of the movement leaders took their signals from the Holy Spirit. The Holy Spirit filled the role of *Superintending Guide* for the apostles' missionary endeavors; He longs to fill that role for us in the twenty-first century as well.

Preparer for the Future

That the Holy Spirit would reveal the future to Jesus' followers is in total alignment with Jesus' Upper Room teaching on the Holy Spirit. Just prior to His arrest and trial, Jesus promised that the Holy Spirit would tell them what was yet to come (see John 16:13). Literally, He would serve Jesus' followers as the "Preparer for the Future." Concrete illustrations of the Holy Spirit revealing the future includes when: the Holy Spirit predicted famine through Agabus (see Acts 11:28). He also provided warning of impending danger for the apostle Paul (see Acts 20:23; 21:11).

Often the Holy Spirit fills our hearts with strong impressions about the hours, days, and weeks ahead. In so doing, He prepares us to face danger, to take preventive action, or to change the direction of our course. The Holy Spirit clearly warned that *"in latter times some will abandon the faith and follow deceiving spirits and things taught by demons"* (1 Timothy 4:1). This was none other than the Holy Spirit filling the role of "Preparer for the Future."

Church Missionaries Commissioned

The Holy Spirit initiated and superintended the commissioning of the first missionaries to the Gentile world (see Acts 13:1-4). God the Son had given clear instructions to the apostles and to us to be His witnesses in Jerusalem, Judea, Samaria, and the uttermost parts of the earth. Now, the Holy Spirit was moving the church in Antioch to obey Jesus' clear command. Luke tells us that the Holy Spirit spoke clearly to the prophets, teachers, and members of the Antioch church with specific instructions to send designated people on a specific mission. Did they hear an actual audible voice? There may well have been such a voice allowing all to hear the same instructions simultaneously. I appreciate Luke's silence on the means the Holy Spirit chose to communicate His instructions. What we do know is that the five prophets and teachers, and the congregation as well, were all convinced that the Holy Spirit had spoken. There was immediate unity over what the Holy Spirit had said. We can confidently add that whenever the Holy Spirit speaks and we obey there will always be unity and never discord.

Although both leaders and members of the church at Antioch were directly involved in the commissioning of the first two Christian missionaries into the Gentile World, it is also clear that this venture was initiated and directed by the Holy Spirit (see Acts 13:4). The primary role of the church at Antioch was to create an atmosphere through worship, prayer, fasting, and prompt obedience into which the Holy Spirit could speak with clarity and power. That, by the way, is still the primary role of the local church in the commissioning of missionaries to engage in cross-cultural ministry.

Unity in Cultural Diversity

The Holy Spirit bridged the gap between Jews and Gentiles (see Acts 15:8-11). He indwelt and empowered both Jews and Gentiles, two culturally and religiously diverse peoples. The Holy Spirit did not favor one group over the other. He guided the church to a conclusion that avoided division. Our responsibility is to

> Our responsibility is to maintain the unity created by the Holy Spirit.

maintain the unity created by the Holy Spirit. We cannot create the unity of the Spirit, but we can preserve the precious gift of unity.

Unity in Theological Diversity

The Holy Spirit superintended the discussion at the Jerusalem Council and guided the leaders to adopt a flexible, reasonable, and contextualized approach to launching a CPM in the Gentile world (see Acts 15:28). Together the leaders discerned the will of the Holy Spirit in the matters of dispute. The division revolved around the insistence by the Judaisers that Gentile believers must be circumcised. Had this group prevailed, the expansion of the church into the Gentile world would have been hindered, and perhaps even halted. What a critical moment this was for the church! The Holy Spirit preserved both unity and order.

Church Leaders Appointed

The Holy Spirit appointed overseers for each local church (Acts 20:28). Paul was confident that it was the Holy Spirit who had chosen the elders to lead the church at Ephesus. He took the appointment of local church leaders very seriously. He did not rely on his own instinct to identify and choose the right leaders. For this reason Paul and Barnabas appointed elders in every church with prayer and fasting (see Acts 14:23).

Conclusion

Among the many varied tasks of the Holy Spirit in the Book of Acts, we note the following: He *empowered* the leaders to lead, *emboldened* ordinary men to preach fearlessly, added *persuasiveness* and *conviction* to the apostles' preaching, provided precise *guidance* for the leaders of the first CPM, protected the church from *bogging down* into legalism, and helped with the *selection* of new leaders. It was utterly unthinkable then, as well as today, to attempt launching a CPM without the divine Superintendent. In the Acts account, the Holy Spirit *spoke continually;*

filled or *controlled* the followers of Jesus; was *poured out* on Jesus' followers; *convicted* the hearers of the truth of the gospel; was given as a *gift* by the Father; could be *lied to, tested* and *resisted;* could be *received; spoke through* human spokespersons; *restrained and constrained* Jesus' followers; *compelled and warned; and appointed leaders.*

My concluding question is this: Is the Holy Spirit active in all we do? Will we allow Him to work today like He did in the Book of Acts? Dare we hinder Him? Oh, for the conscious, complete, and continuous control of the Holy Spirit over every ministry initiative, strategy, and plan.

Prayer

Holy Spirit of counsel and power, You dwell within me as my Superintending Guide. Only You can help me understand and follow the Father's ways. Only You know and reveal the Father's thoughts. Only with Your energizing power and Your superintending guidance can I fulfill the Father's eternal purposes.

You are the Executor of plans made in the eternal councils of the Holy Trinity. In the beginning You brooded over all of God's Creation in its dark and chaotic state. You brought order to all that Jesus Christ, the living Word, spoke into existence.

When the eternal Son of God came to earth as our Emmanuel, You superintended the miracle of His virgin birth, hovered over Him at His baptism, and led Him into the wilderness to be tempted by Satan. You empowered Jesus to proclaim the good news and to drive out demons. After Jesus' death, burial, resurrection, and ascension to the Father's right hand, You took His place here on earth as our Comforting Counselor.

As You watched over the early church, energizing and guiding Jesus' followers, You now superintend all kingdom ventures launched by Your missionary servants. Your direction and Your power have neither been withdrawn nor diminished since the days of that early church. You are still the Superintending Guide of all missionary endeavors; You are the Spirit of counsel and of power for all of Your "international harvesters" everywhere. Whether our church planting endeavors take us into modern world-class cities or to primitive jungle dwellers, into countries that welcome us or into places that are hostile toward Christian missionaries, You are still our Superintending Guide.

The very notion that we could complete the Great Commission apart from Your strength and direction is arrogant presumption. You sovereignly orchestrate the giving of spiritual gifts to plant and water the church. You have generously given workers to serve the church as apostles, prophets, evangelists, and pastor-teachers. Whatever our task as missionaries, we confess our need of Your power to energize us, Your counsel to guide us, and Your joy to strengthen us.

You nudge us and prompt us daily in the direction of the Father's eternal purposes. You direct our steps along the path of the sovereign Lord's perfect will. Superintending Guide, we desperately need Your conscious, continuous, and complete control over every thought, conversation, motivation, and attitude. Amen.

THE HOLY SPIRIT AS MY REVEALER OF THE FUTURE

Just hours before His trial and crucifixion, Jesus gave the Twelve His final and most comprehensive teaching on the Holy Spirit. You already have in hand four essays on the Holy Spirit based on Jesus' Upper Room teaching. In them we considered the following four roles of the Holy Spirit:

- The Holy Spirit as our Comforting Counselor (see John 14:16-18)
- The Holy Spirit as our Resident Rabbi (see John 14:26)
- The Holy Spirit as our Convincing Apologist (see John 15:26-27)
- The Holy Spirit as our Convicting Evangelist (see John 16:7-11)

In this essay we have another important piece on Jesus' Upper Room teaching on the Holy Spirit. I shall follow my usual format of exegeting the text followed by personal application. As you read what follows, keep in mind that intimacy with God is possible only with the help of the Holy Spirit.

We must not lose sight of the context of Jesus' teaching on the Holy Spirit. He is in the Upper Room giving final instruction to His distraught disciples. His repeated statements about His impending death and resurrection made no sense to them. His statements did not fit their future with Jesus and the visible, earthly kingdom they expected Him to establish very soon. Only after Jesus' resurrection did they understand that the death of Jesus was neither an execution nor a suicide. The underlying reason for His substitutionary, sacrificial death was to make atonement for the sins of the world.

"I have much more to say to you, more than you can now bear" (John 16:12).

For three years Jesus had taught His disciples, sometimes in a private setting and at other times with the crowds listening in. Now, He had come to the end of His time with them; He was returning to the Father who had sent Him. Although there was much more that Jesus longed to share with His followers, He must leave that to the Holy Spirit of truth. Jesus was being sensitive to their capacity to take in more teaching, teaching that would have crushed them beneath its weight. Even hearing Jesus say moments earlier that He was returning to the Father had filled their hearts with grief (John 16:6). These were extremely emotional moments for the disciples.

"But when he, the Spirit of truth, comes, he will guide you into all truth" (John 16:13).

Jesus kept referring to a time when the Holy Spirit would come. The disciples knew about the Holy Spirit, but clearly Jesus was promising that very soon a major change in the Holy Spirit's relationship to them would occur. We now know what that change was. Exactly fifty days between the Passover Feast and the Feast of Pentecost, the Holy Spirit was "poured out" on a band of waiting, obedient, praying disciples. Let us not forget that there in the Upper Room with Jesus, the disciples did not have this information. Like us, they were near-sighted and could not see the future. God has not created us to see the future without divine help.

All that the Holy Spirit would teach the disciples about Jesus would be true. He would ensure that all of Jesus' followers, including us centuries later, would be protected from erroneous conclusions about Jesus. The work of the Holy Spirit would be to help Jesus' followers to comprehend and

> We need the Spirit of truth, our *Resident Rabbi* to guide us to the truth about Jesus.

apply the truth and ultimately to "bow the knee" to the truth. Because we will never in a thousand lifetimes discover the truth about Jesus on our own, we need the Spirit of truth, our *Resident Rabbi,* to guide us to the truth about Jesus.

There are many spirits in the world, but only one Holy Spirit. There are many spirits, but only one Spirit of truth. Jesus Himself designated the Holy Spirit as the Spirit of truth. He promised His followers that the Spirit of truth would guide them into all truth. His chief concern is the truth about Jesus Christ the eternal Son of God.

This process of being guided into the truth is lifelong. Those who are filled or controlled by the Holy Spirit have been guided into more and more truth over the past year, perhaps even over the past week. Through the guiding work of the Holy Spirit, we comprehend more and more of God's eternal truth. As our comprehension grows, so does our capacity (our hunger) to take in more of God's truth.

Although God's final Word has been spoken through His Son and through His written Word in the Bible, meaning that there will be no further written revelation, we have not come anywhere near comprehending all of God's Holy Word. The work of our *Resident Rabbi* is to continually guide us into more of the truth already given to us in the Scriptures.

"He will not speak on his own; he will speak only what he hears, and he will tell you what is yet to come" (John 16:13).

Here is a most unselfish thing. The Holy Spirit does not have an independent message of His own. He will never veer from the teaching Jesus had already given to His followers. He will not invent new words or new ideas. He is not the Author of new theologies. He will not set aside the Scriptures and strike out on a course of His own. Jesus assured the disciples that the message the Holy Spirit hears from the Father and from the Son is also the message He would share with them. The Holy Spirit will never pursue an agenda of His own.

I am personally fascinated and moved by Jesus' further words about the Holy Spirit's teaching role. Jesus promised that He would tell Jesus' followers *"what is yet to come."* Is this a reference to end time events like the Rapture, the judgment seat of Christ, or the Great White Throne Judgment? Is Jesus speaking generally of all that would one day come to pass in accordance with the Scriptures? Clearly, that must be what Jesus was saying. We know that the Gospel writers, the apostles—Paul, Peter, John, Jude and others—all spoke about the end times, including the second coming of Jesus Christ. The apostle John whom Jesus loved was listening to Jesus' teaching in the Upper Room. At this time, he had no idea that he would become the human author of the Revelation, which deals almost entirely with the future.

Anyone who desires to be a student of prophetic Scripture needs the help of the Holy Spirit. To Him has been committed the task of revealing to us *"what is yet to come."* What comfort to know that we have not been left to grope about in the dark regarding the future! This applies to the immediate and distant future.

None of the disciples listening to Jesus there in the Upper Room knew about the outpouring of the Holy Spirit on the day of Pentecost in fifty days, of the literal fulfillment of the Great Commission on the day of Pentecost (Acts 2:5-6), of the impending destruction of Jerusalem in AD 70 at the cruel hand of Titus, or of the spread of the gospel to the Gentile world, but the Holy Spirit knew all this. It was His task to prepare Jesus' followers for these and other future events.

Jesus did not want His followers to stumble aimlessly into the future. That would have been disastrous. He was giving His disciples the *Revealer of the Future* so that they could walk into the unknown with confidence. As the leaders of the early church faced an unknown future, the Holy Spirit prepared them for it.

> Two thousand years later, we can see how precisely the Holy Spirit prepared the church for its future.

Two thousand years later, we can see how precisely the Holy Spirit prepared the church for its future. Even today in the twenty-first century He is preparing the church for certain perilous days ahead. We do not know how much future remains before the Lord returns, but Jesus assured us that the Holy Spirit would help us to be ready for whatever the future brings to us. There is nothing more frightening than uncertainty about the future. The ambiguity about not knowing the future can fill our hearts with a sense of foreboding. Praise be to God for giving us the Holy Spirit whose task it is to prepare the church for the final days just ahead.

We must not think that the Holy Spirit's role of preparing us for the future is limited to end-time events. As we walk in the Spirit, keep in step with the Spirit, and live under His control, He prompts us and nudges us to make decisions that fit the future with precision. When the future is overtaken by the present, we look back in amazement over the accuracy with which the Holy Spirit helped us to choose just the right course of action. We know that we could never have made such good decisions on our own. As missionary servants of the Lord, we are assured that God's preferred future is always the future the Holy Spirit prepares us for. The wonderful thing is that we can ask the Holy Spirit to "write" God's preferred future onto our hearts and then guide us steadily toward implementing it.

Jesus' promise that the Holy Spirit will tell us what is yet to come could also apply to the whole development of the Christian Church. When Jesus shared His teaching on the Holy Spirit, the church had not yet been born. As we move into the Acts of the Apostles, it becomes quickly apparent that the disciples were "building the road they were walking on." Step-by-step, the Holy Spirit guided them into the right shape of the church. He prepared them for the intense persecution and fierce opposition they would face. He guided them into new structures. He also led them to adopt new initiatives like the mission to the Gentiles.

I distinctly recall during my teenage years being gripped by a foreboding sense of anxiety over the future. Listening to adults' conversations led me to the conclusion that our world had spun out of control and that doomsday was imminent. What I saw and heard created an atmosphere of pessimistic gloom. More specifically, I was fearful that in a time of persecution or tribulation, I would deny my Lord like Peter did. More than anything else, I wanted to remain true to my Lord. Then in my mid-teens, the Holy Spirit guided me into a truth that has remained with me for more than five decades. My *Comforting Counselor* helped me to understand that nothing, not even "things to come," would be able to separate me from the love of God (Romans 8:35ff.). I need not fear the future; it was secure in the hand of almighty God!

"He will bring glory to me by taking from what is mine and making it known to you" (John 16:14).

The work of the Holy Spirit is to honor, glorify, and magnify the Lord Jesus Christ. The Holy Spirit's concern is not His own prominence; His desire is to exalt the person of Jesus Christ. His goal is to make Jesus the center of our thoughts, the focus of our service. Literally, the Holy Spirit will praise Jesus the Son by helping us to understand Jesus' teaching. We noted above that what He teaches is not about Himself but about

Jesus. Here we note that what He promotes is not about Himself, but again about Jesus.

The work of the Holy Spirit is Christocentric, never Spirit-centric. The Holy Spirit will never lead a church or a church's leadership team to focus on Himself to the exclusion of Jesus Christ. We could add that neither will He allow the church's leaders to usurp Jesus' glory. In summary, the Holy Spirit will take what is true about Jesus and make it known to His followers. We can count on the Spirit of truth to teach Jesus' followers only the truth about Jesus.

"All that belongs to the Father is mine. That is why I said the Spirit will take from what is mine and make it known to you" (John 16:15).

Note the joint ownership between the Father and the Son. There is much we do not understand about the Trinity, but it is certain that there is perfect unity and never competition within the Godhead. It is the truth that belongs jointly to the Father and the Son that the Holy Spirit will reveal to Jesus' followers.

Application

We have already touched on some application to Jesus' teaching on the Holy Spirit as recorded by the apostle John. Please note the following summary points of additional application:

- Part of the Holy Spirit's role is to prepare Jesus' followers for the future, both near and distant.
- The focus of the Holy Spirit is never Himself, but always on the Lord Jesus Christ.
- Being guided into all truth is a lifelong process. We could not bear receiving all of the truth about Jesus Christ at one time. The truth must be applied to developing an intimate walk with God. That's what takes so much time.

Prayer

Holy Spirit of God, as my Comforting Counselor You mediate the presence of the Father and the Son to me. As my Resident Rabbi You live within me and remind me continually of Jesus' teaching; as my Convincing Apologist You build an irrefutable case for Jesus Christ as the eternal Son of God; and as my Convicting Evangelist You draw the lost of our world to the Savior.

I yield myself to Your control to receive Your comfort and counsel in times of heaviness, Your instruction to understand and apply Jesus' teaching, Your witness to Jesus as the Son of God, and Your guilty verdict on the lost who reject Jesus.

Gracious Holy Spirit, You are also the Revealer of Our Future. I am comforted by Jesus' promise that You will tell us "what is yet to come." As the Revealer of Our Future, You inspired prophets and apostles to write about the imminent return of Jesus. We do not expect additional written revelations about Jesus' second coming, but we do need Your help to understand the end time teaching You have already inspired.

As for my ability to know the future, I confess that I am incurably nearsighted. Even tomorrow is beyond my vision to know with certainty. Spirit of wisdom and understanding, of counsel and power, take the Father's plans and purposes for the days ahead and write them on the "tablet" of my heart. Prepare me for the uncertainties, dangers, and ambiguities in my future. Help me with decisions that have lasting ramifications on into the future.

It is not a premonition or a stronger sixth sense that we rely on. Instead we need to sense Your promptings and Your nudgings onto the path marked out for us. I need Your guidance into a course of action that prepares me for Your preferred future. Amen.

THE HOLY SPIRIT AS MY PERSISTENT GARDENER

But the fruit of the Spirit *is love, joy, peace, patience, kindness, goodness, faithfulness, gentleness, and self-control. Against such things there is no law.* (Galatians 5:22-23, emphasis added*)*

The Christian is a divine work in process, a work of the Holy Spirit whose lifelong goal is to transform the child of God into the image of Jesus Christ. This progressive process is usually referred to as the sanctification of the believer. Sanctification begins with the new birth and continues till the day the Lord welcomes us into His eternal presence. The ultimate product of this sanctification process is Christ-likeness.

Becoming more and more like the Lord Jesus Christ is yet another way of expressing the overall theme of this series of essays on intimacy with God.

With the Galatians 5:22-23 text in mind, I like to think of the Holy Spirit as my *Persistent Gardener* and that I, in turn, am His "orchard." With great patience and perseverance, He "cultivates," "waters," and "prunes" His orchard. The Holy Spirit begins this work of tending His orchard the very moment He takes up His residence in me; He continues His work as my *Persistent Gardener* 24–7 till the day I stand in the presence of the Lord Jesus Christ.

How does He cultivate, prune, and water His orchard? He takes full advantage of trying relationships, challenging ministry assignments, financial losses, and even chronic physical ailments through which to bear in us the fruit of Christ-like character traits. When we face these challenging tests, we can ask ourselves, what would Jesus do, what would Jesus say, or how would Jesus react? Not only does the Holy Spirit take advantage of our day-to-day circumstances to produce Christlikeness in us, He sovereignly orchestrates them to bear the maximum amount of His beautiful fruit.

Now, let us examine the context for this text on the Holy Spirit and intimacy with God.

The Holy Spirit's Lifelong Battle with Our Sinful Nature
(Galatians 5:16-18)

The indwelling Holy Spirit is actively and aggressively pitted against the sinful nature residing in us. His opposition to the acts of our sinful nature amounts to all-out war. There can never be a truce between the Holy Spirit dwelling in us and our sinful nature also residing in us. They are diametrically opposed to each other, totally incompatible with each other. A comparison of the acts of our sinful nature and the fruit of the Holy Spirit gives us a clear picture of their stark difference. The relentless, fierce struggle between these two enemies will continue unabated till the day we die.

> The Holy Spirit's daily goal is to transform us more and more into the likeness of Jesus Christ.

The Holy Spirit's daily goal is to transform us more and more into the likeness of Jesus Christ. Our sinful nature, on the other hand, lures us, entices us, and tempts us in just the opposite direction—away from the desires of the Holy Spirit toward the natural inclinations of our sin nature. This is not to say that the Holy Spirit and our sinful nature are equal in strength and that the outcome of this struggle is in doubt. Thanks be to God! The Holy Spirit is ultimately and decisively the Victor.

In this fierce struggle between the Holy Spirit and our sinful nature, we must not view ourselves as passive bystanders. We must take sides; we cannot remain neutral. For the Holy Spirit to triumph in this struggle we must consciously hand over complete control of our lives to Him. Whether we walk in the Spirit or give in to the flesh is a choice we make numerous times every day. I personally pray every day for the conscious, continuous, complete control of the Holy Spirit. This prayer reflects the attitude of my heart of submission to the Holy Spirit throughout each day. I long to have my *Persistent Gardener* take charge of my thoughts, attitudes, motivations, conversations, choice of words, and decisions.

Overcoming the Sinful Nature (Galatians 5:16, 25)

The bottom line question is simply this: "To whom do we give way—to the Holy Spirit in us or to our sinful nature in us?" Of course, the easiest course of action is to allow our sinful nature to dominate our attitudes, conversations, and conduct. Capitulation to the sinful nature is our most natural course of action. As a falling object is pulled downward by the law of gravity, our natural direction, our natural inclination, our propensity is toward alignment with our sinful nature.

How then do we overcome the daily onslaught of temptations to speak unkind words; to think unholy, unclean thoughts; and to commit sinful acts? Is it really possible to become more like Christ? If so, how? How do we shed the shackles of our sinful nature's bondage? How can we triumph over habits that have long plagued us, even to the point of despair? Is it really possible to achieve and enjoy daily intimacy with God?

With such a set of complex questions, surely the answer is also very complicated. Not so! The secret to victory is the Holy Spirit's control over our sinful nature. Alone, we are no match for the strong tug of our sinful nature. The Holy Spirit stands ready to deliver us from the subjugation of our sinful natures. As we *"live by the Spirit"* (5:16), or as "we *keep in step with the Spirit"* (5:25), we will *"not gratify the desires of the sinful nature"* (5:16).

As the Holy Spirit is allowed to control or fill us, the sinful *"acts of the sinful nature"* (5:19) lose both their appeal and their power. As we yield to the Holy Spirit, He will produce in us a most attractive list of character traits of Christlikeness known as the "fruit of the Spirit." We must choose between the control of the Spirit, with His nine-fold fruit of Christlikeness, and the acts of our sinful nature. The choice is also between the domination of our sinful nature and its long list of odious and destructive acts.

Imagine for a moment, the difference in marriages, friendships, board meetings, or strategic planning sessions, where the Holy Spirit is allowed to bear His nine-fold fruit of love, joy, peace, patience, kindness, goodness, faithfulness, gentleness, and self-control. Imagine the powerful, far-reaching impact of the Spirit's control over a missionary's life and ministry. What beauty! What attraction! What winsomeness! What unity!

The Acts of the Sinful Nature (Galatians 5:19-21)

Paul makes clear that the list of 15 "acts of the sinful nature" listed in our text represent but a partial list. The list is closer to complete if we add the sins in such parallel texts as Mark 7:21-23, 1 Corinthians 6:9-10, Ephesians 5:3-5, 2 Timothy 3:2-5, and Malachi 3:5.

Combining all of these texts, we have the following frightening list of sins committed by the sinful nature, all sins against which the Holy Spirit wages relentless war. I suggest that you read the list slowly and contemplatively, allowing the heinous nature of each sin to sink in. Jesus died to save us from this catalogue of sinful acts; the Holy Spirit fills us to defeat them: *Sexual immorality, impurity, idolatry, hatred, fits of rage, jealousy, selfish ambition, dissension, homosexuality, drunkenness, silly-*

talk, greed, evil thoughts, theft, not loving good, pride, ungratefulness, deceit, treacherousness, prostitution, lack of self-control, scoffing, fault finding, rashness, love of self, unloving, love of money, malice, abusive behavior, perjury, unholiness, brutality, unforgiving attitude, grumbling, inflating the price, murder, disobedience, slander, using deceptive packaging, cheating with dishonest scales, and witchcraft.

These are the sins that destroy marriages, divide churches, undermine friendships, and ultimately destroy societies. These are the sins that dog our steps to our dying day. They should not, need not, be allowed to gain the mastery over us, however. The Spirit-filled, Spirit-controlled Christian will avoid the pitfalls of all of these "acts of the sinful nature."

My inner reaction to the above list is one of revulsion. There is absolutely no way I could take on even a few of these sins in my own strength. I need the Holy Spirit's help. I must consciously, intentionally give way to the Holy Spirit to avoid the evil deeds of my sinful nature. I offer deep thanks to God the Father and to God the Son for giving me the Holy Spirit to overcome my sinful nature's list of evil acts, and beyond that to bear through me His beautiful fruit of love.

The Fruit of the Spirit (Galatians 5:22-23)

Note that the apostle Paul speaks of the Spirit's fruit in the singular. The implication is that there is but one fruit, a nine-fold cluster of the fruit of love. The love born in us by the Holy Spirit is other-centered, unconditional, and eternal. It is the love Jesus demonstrated through His sacrificial, substitutionary death on the cross. It is the love described in the love chapter (1 Corinthians 13). It is the love that spends itself at the expense of itself for the sake of others. It is the love a Spirit-filled, Spirit-controlled child of God exhibits through his/her attitudes, motivations, words, and actions.

As we consider this attractive cluster of fruit, we discover, as we have already pointed out numerous times in this essay, that we are really describing Jesus' beautiful character. The more we allow the Holy Spirit to develop this cluster of fruit in us, the more we will reflect the beauty of Jesus Christ.

LOVE: *The Spirit-filled Christian obeys the Great Commandment by loving God passionately and people compassionately.*

JOY: *The Spirit-filled Christian lives confidently above adverse circumstances.*

PEACE: *The Spirit-filled Christian pursues and enjoys harmony with God and with man.*

PATIENCE: *The Spirit-filled Christian responds graciously under pressure to retaliate.*

KINDNESS: *The Spirit-filled Christian demonstrates humble restraint and courageous action.*

GOODNESS: *The Spirit-filled Christian champions all that is good and rejects all that is evil.*

FAITHFULNESS: *The Spirit-filled Christian serves both God and man dependably and loyally.*

GENTLENESS: *The Spirit-filled Christian speaks and acts appropriately without a hurtful edge.*

SELF-CONTROL: *The Spirit-filled Christian overcomes all self-gratifying, fleshly appetites.*

Application

What power, what magnetism, what beauty there is in a life through which the Holy Spirit bears His nine-fold fruit of love! This fruit is totally foreign to our world. We must remind ourselves continually that this fruit is not the Christian's fruit. On the contrary, it is the fruit of the Holy Spirit, our *Persistent Gardener*. It is certainly not our winsome charm or our pleasing personality that attracts lost people into the Kingdom of God. No, no! It is the Holy Spirit's fruit that the Christian can bear in greater and greater abundance. The challenge before all of us is to allow the Holy Spirit to turn our lives into a fruitful orchard in which grows the beautiful fruit of love, joy, peace, patience, kindness, goodness, faithfulness, gentleness, and self-control.

Prayer

Gracious Holy Spirit, my Persistent Gardener, I am Your "orchard" to cultivate, water, and prune. Your daily desire is to bear in me a cluster of the character traits of Jesus. Your lifelong, persistent goal is to transform me more and more into the image of my Lord.

I invite You to use every relationship, both enjoyable and difficult, each challenging ministry assignment, and all trying circumstances to bear in me increasingly more of the likeness of Christ Jesus, my Lord. I recognize my part is to submit to Your control, to allow You to fill me and to empower me, to respond obediently to Your prompting, and to remain in step with Your leading.

In addition to bearing Your fruit in us, You have generously given each of us ministry gifts with which to build up the body of Christ. None of us has all of your spiritual gifts, but through Your work as our Persistent Gardener, each of us can bear an abundance of Your fruit. With Your patient persistence, You produce in us more and more of the nine-fold fruit of Christ-likeness.

How sad if I possess prominent spiritual gifts for public service but lack the fruit of Christlikeness to beautify them. Dear Holy Spirit, Your fruit of love makes Your ministry gifts more attractive to those I serve. Your fruit of love creates harmonious relationships within Christ's body. Your fruit of love beautifies my marriage and all of my friendships. Your fruit of love in us draws sinners to the Savior of the world.

As the Persistent Gardener in my life, I yield myself to You to bear a bumper crop of the nine-fold fruit of love, joy, peace, patience, kindness, goodness, faithfulness, gentleness, and self-control. I ask for this cluster of wonderful fruit for the glory of God. Amen.

THE HOLY SPIRIT AS MY PATIENT INTERCESSOR

In the same way, the Spirit helps us in our weakness. We do not know what we ought to pray for, but the Spirit himself intercedes for us with groans that words cannot express. And he who searches our hearts knows the mind of the Spirit, because the Spirit intercedes for the saints in accordance with God's will. (Romans 8:26-27)

Who among us has not lamented weakness in prayer; struggled with wandering thoughts; felt smitten with guilt over an erratic prayer life; or like Peter, James, and John in the Garden of Gethsemane, succumbed to drowsiness? It may be true after all that prayer is the final discipline for the mature Christian to learn.

Jesus' disciples recognized their deficiency in prayer, probably because they compared it to Jesus' consistent, intimate communion with the Father. On at least one occasion, they asked Him to teach them how to pray like John the Baptizer had taught his disciples (Luke 11:1). The clear implication is that the art of prayer must be learned. No one comes by prayer naturally or easily. Neither Hudson Taylor, George

Mueller, or Praying Hyde became prayer warriors in the early days of their missionary ministry. They learned prayer over the years.

Jesus responded to the disciples' plea for lessons on prayer by telling them what to say each time they prayed. He did not say that every time they prayed, they should utter the same words in rote fashion. Rather, the model prayer Jesus gave His disciples was intended to list the categories to be covered in our prayers. Of course, within each of these prayer categories there is room for spontaneity. Although not exhaustive, they form a well-rounded prayer outline:

- A foundational Father/child relationship
- Worship/adoration toward the Father
- Rule, reign, and lordship of the Father
- Petition the Father for daily, temporal needs
- Confession of sin to the Father
- Forgiveness of others' wrongs
- Victory over temptation by the evil one.

As early as my teen years, the model prayer Jesus gave His followers became my prayer paradigm. Although I have resorted to a few other prayer outlines for comparatively short periods of time, I keep returning to the prayer categories Jesus gave His disciples. Circumstances are sure to change, sometimes daily, but the prayer categories Jesus gave us do not; they are enduring and comprehensive enough to last a lifetime. A good practice is to pray your way through the seven-point prayer outline.

> Our *Patient Intercessor* is intensely engaged with us each time we pray.

The Holy Spirit, our *Patient Intercessor,* is intensely engaged with us each time we pray. That our Lord Jesus Christ is our Intercessor at the right hand of the Father is a truth widely taught among us. We revel in His continuous intercessory ministry on our behalf. But that the Holy Spirit is our *Patient Intercessor* residing in us here on earth is not emphasized as much as it should be. Whereas the Son prays to the Father *for us*, the Holy Spirit prays to Him *in us*. Earlier in this series of essays on the Holy Spirit and intimacy with God, we discovered that the Holy Spirit is our *Resident Rabbi*; that is, He helps us to understand and apply Jesus' teaching. Now we note that the Holy Spirit is also our *Patient Intercessor* in that He prompts and nudges us both to know how to pray as well as what to pray. The Christian never prays alone. Our *Patient Intercessor* in us is always right there praying in us, with us, and through us.

The Holy Spirit Aids Us in Our Prayers

Our text informs us that the Holy Spirit helps us in our weakness. To be sure, He assists us in every kind of weakness, but since the context of His help here is prayer, we conclude that He specifically aids us in our limitations in prayer. Our weakness in prayer is multi-faceted. Left alone, we pray with limited perspective, limited energy, limited concern, and limited concentration. The Holy Spirit enlarges our perspective to comprehend the perfect will of God. He puts words of praise, adoration, and intercession onto our lips. He replaces our weakness of body with renewed vigor. He stirs in us a heart-hunger and a soul-thirst for almighty God. In other words, He creates in us both a *desire* for God and a *delight* in God. He keeps our otherwise wandering minds focused on the Father for extended periods of time. Our Global Concerts of Prayer would have been sheer drudgery apart from the energizing help of the Holy Spirit.

Our greatest weakness in prayer is our inability to know the future. Should we pray for healing or for grace to cope with an illness or even for death? Should we wait for a certain relationship to develop, or should we wait for another person to come into our lives? Should we focus our energies and our time on reaching this unreached people group or on yet another?

We have the promise that the Holy Spirit will help us with decisions related to the future. How does He help us? Our *Patient Intercessor* quickens our minds with thoughts, plans, and solutions. He sorts and sifts through all of the possibilities; He makes sense out of what to us makes absolutely no sense. He brings order out of our inner confusion. With His help, our inarticulate mumblings become clearly crafted petitions. In the end it is as though our prayers blast through all barriers into the light. Where did this help come from? From the Holy Spirit who aids us in our prayer limitations.

> With His help, our inarticulate mumblings become clearly crafted petitions.

One of the most enjoyable applications of the Holy Spirit's aid in prayer has been His writing of sentence prayers on the *"walls of my heart"*—prayers that are brief, focused on specific themes, and that have become part of my daily prayer repertoire. These shorter prayers are like my soul's daily agenda. They are Spirit-prompted petitions that I would never have thought of praying to the Father. One of the advantages of this repertoire of sentence prayers is that available time can determine how long I have to devote to them. With more time, a sentence prayer can easily be expanded into a paragraph or two of communion with God, but used while driving or exercising, the short version works well. Here are a few examples of short prayers I personally use:

- **Hunger and Thirst for God:** *Loving Lord, stir in me a heart-hunger that only You can satisfy and a soul-thirst that only You can quench.* Although only one sentence in length, this prayer reminds me that intimacy with God is hunger and thirst driven and that the most frightening state for the believer to fall into is apathy. I pray this prayer more often than any other.
- **Communion with God:** *Gracious God, as I open Your eternal Word this morning, grant me Your Holy Spirit to open my eyes to see*

Your beauty, unstop my ears to hear You speak, illumine my mind to understand and apply Your truth, and move my heart to obey You eagerly. My full expectation is that God will answer this prayer and that I will indeed see the beauty of my Lord; hear His voice with my inner ears; understand His unchanging, incorruptible Word; and obey the eternal Word of God without hesitation.

- **Intimacy with God:** *Faithful Father, prosper my daily quest for intimacy with You; help me today to go progressively deeper in knowing You, loving You, and serving You.* I am very passionate about this prayer. It is a daily confession that without the Holy Spirit's help, intimacy with God is an impossibility.

- **Control of the Holy Spirit:** *Gracious God, I ask for the conscious, complete, continuous control of Your Holy Spirit over all of my thoughts, attitudes, motivations, conversations, and decisions.* What I am asking for in this daily prayer is the fullness of the Holy Spirit. With rare exception, this is a prayer the Holy Spirit prompts me to pray multiple times a day.

- **Nine-fold Fruit of the Spirit:** *Holy Spirit of God, today (in this situation) bear in me Your nine-fold fruit of Christlike character traits: love, joy, peace, patience, kindness, goodness, faithfulness, gentleness, and self-control.* I find myself dwelling longer on the fruit I am least likely to bear. There is in me a reluctance to employ the gifts of the Spirit without the beautifying impact of the fruit of the Spirit.

- **Public Preaching/Teaching:** *My Lord, as I preach/teach the Word today, grant me joy, liberty, passion, power, a conscious sense of Your presence, and fruit that will last.* I utter this prayer often in anticipation of a public preaching or teaching opportunity. Frequently the Holy Spirit prompts this prayer the very moment I am taking my place behind the pulpit to deliver a message. I have also asked others to pray this very prayer for me as I stand before an audience to share God's message.

- **Evangelism:** *Merciful Master, today help me to be Your evangelist by recognizing and taking advantage of witnessing opportunities orchestrated by Your Holy Spirit.* My personal commitment is to share a verbal witness in all situations where the Holy Spirit Himself orchestrates a witnessing opportunity. There is great joy in allowing the Holy Spirit to create the opportunities to engage in evangelism.

The Holy Spirit Aligns Our Prayers with the Father's Perfect Will

Not only does the Holy Spirit aid us in our limitations in prayer, He also brings our prayers into complete alignment with the will of the Father.

Our *Patient Intercessor* may do His work of alignment by reminding us of a passage of Scripture that leads us to understand and submit to God's perfect will. He may choose to use the exhortation of a brother or sister to bring us into compliance with God's will. Alternately, He may convict us of an attitude problem as we relive a conversation that took place earlier in the day. His means are many, but His single goal is to bring us into compliance with the *plumb line* of God's standard, the written Word of God.

Our thinking, our attitude, and even the direction we have chosen could all be in serious misalignment. On our own, we could be veering dangerously off course, but while at prayer, the Holy Spirit changes our minds, tempers our attitudes, and adjusts our direction. These mid-course corrections come in the form of promptings and urgings from the Holy Spirit. His goal is to keep us in perfect alignment with the Father's will. He "writes" the perfect plan of God onto the "tablets" of our hearts. The thoughts, plans, strategic goals, and faith objectives that come from the Holy Spirit will be in total agreement with the eternal purposes of God.

Application

None of us can claim to understand prayer fully. It will no doubt always remain a mystery, at least in part. Let us not be vexed over those facets of prayer that we do not understand. Rather, let us focus on those aspects of prayer that seem clear from Scripture. For example, it is clear that when it comes to prayer, we are weak, even feeble. We have chosen to use the word "limited," applying it to the weaknesses in our prayer life. It is also very clear that the Holy Spirit helps us in our limitations. He helps us to know what to pray and how to pray. He puts words into our mouths, words we can use in our prayer to God. He understands the language of groans and sighs. He takes these inarticulate expressions and fashions them into prayers to the Father—prayers that are in sync with the Father's perfect will.

Prayer

Spirit of the living God, You dwell within me as my Patient Intercessor.

Whenever I pray, You come to my aid. You also align my prayers with the Sovereign Lord's eternal purposes. You take my wordless-sighs and my pain-filled groans and fashion them into prayers that please the Father. My gracious Lord Jesus, You pray to the Father for me. My Patient Intercessor, You pray to the Father in me.

Spirit of the living God, I confess to huge limitations in my feeble attempts at prayer. For my limited perspective, help me to comprehend the Father's perfect plan. For my toddler-like gibberish, grant me creative expressions to worship and adore my wonderful Lord. For my weary body and drowsy eyes, energize me with Your strength. For limited passion for You, my faithful Father, stir in me a heart-hunger and a soul-thirst. For my limited compassion for the lost, irrigate my arid heart with the Father's love.

Spirit of the living God, the Father searches for intercessors on behalf of those in desperate need of prayer. Prompt me with intercessory prayers for worldwide workers to bring in the harvest. Burden me to pray for the hundreds of millions of Muslims, Hindus, and Buddhists who await their first intelligible presentation of the life-transforming gospel. Write onto my heart petitions for the lost in my family. I purpose also to pray for the leaders of the nations.

Spirit of the living God, help me to pray without ceasing. Stir in my heart an attitude of continual prayer. When I awaken during the night and as I meditate on the living Word of God, stir my heart with a steady stream of intercessory prayers. As I run errands, discuss Your work with Your servants, or write e-mails on my laptop, prompt my heart to pray to the Father, through the Son, and by You, my Patient Intercessor. Amen.

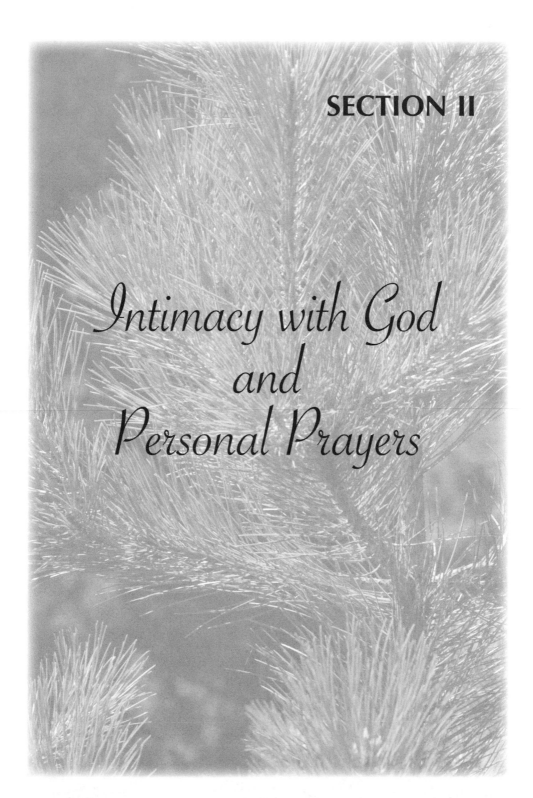

SECTION II

Intimacy with God and Personal Prayers

INTIMACY WITH GOD
AND PERSONAL PRAYERS

One of the new manifestations resulting from an intensified pursuit of intimacy with God was the writing of personal prayers. Initially, I resisted this practice since in my view our prayers to God must be spontaneous. I was quite unaccustomed to praying with my Bible and eyes open, writing and rewriting my prayers to the Father. I came to realize that so-called spontaneous prayers could also be shallow. At the same time, written prayers prompted by the Holy Spirit applying the Scriptures to my life became my soul's delight. I could offer up to the Father prayers that had been Spirit led and biblically based.

I began to use my Cambridge Wide Margin NIV Bible as a place to record many prayers. In time I counted more than three hundred personal prayers in the margins of my Bible.

What comes next in Section II is a sampling of hand-written prayers transcribed from the margins of my Bible to the pages of this book. These prayers have been included as incentive to engage in the soul-satisfying activity of writing your prayers to God. The writing of personal prayers is one way to stoke the fires of intimacy with God.

A PRAYER FOR OBEDIENCE TO THE GREATEST COMMANDMENT

Prompted by Mark 12:30

"Love the Lord your God with all your heart and with all your soul and with all your mind and with all your strength."

Almighty God, loving heavenly Father, You are the Creator of the universe with its billions of galaxies. You are infinitely good and great; I am utterly sinful and small. I marvel that You ask me to love You, that You have made loving You the greatest of all commandments.

The amount of love that flows from one so small to one so great is but a trickle. How could You notice my tiny drop of love in the vast ocean of Your own compassion? Even if I loved You supremely with my entire being, my capacity to love You is utterly microscopic. I do long to love You with the core of my affections, with each of my emotions, with all of my intellectual powers, and with every ounce of my physical strength. Gracious God, enlarge my heart to love You more, stretch my soul to love You more, expand my mind to love You more, and increase my strength to love You more. You desire my first love; You alone deserve all of my first love. As I reflect on my love for You, I am reminded that every bit of love for You originates with You in the first place. Unless the Holy Spirit stirs my heart with a love for You, I will remain totally self-absorbed. Unless the Holy Spirit irrigates my heart with love for You, it remains as dry as a desert in drought.

My Lord, knowing You and loving You must grow together. O, to be completely obedient to this greatest of all commandments. Enlarge my capacity to love You totally; strengthen my resolve to love You supremely. Here in Your holy presence I give myself to a renewed, life-long commitment to go progressively deeper in knowing You, loving You, and serving You.

Amen.

A PRAYER FOR INTIMACY WITH ALMIGHTY GOD

Prompted by Mark 3:35

"Whoever does God's will is my brother and sister and mother."

Faithful Father, sovereign Savior, compassionate Counselor, triune God. You are the God who knows all my passions, my thoughts, and my motivations. You know all about my quest for an intimate walk with You. You planted the longing to seek You into the deepest recesses of my heart. Every inner inclination toward goodness and every desire for holiness comes from You.

My Lord, I lament the snail's pace in this pursuit of intimacy with You. My fervent plea is that You continue to draw me ever nearer to Your side. There is nothing I hunger and thirst for more than to bring personal pleasure to Your heart, to gain insight into Your eternal purposes, to enjoy a conscious sense of Your intimate presence, and to be given frequent glimpses of Your breathtaking beauty.

You have reserved the most intimate of relationships for those who obey You. My Lord, with my whole being I desire to be among those who always obey You. I shall pursue the fulfillment of Your purpose with a holy passion. I resolve to embrace it tightly with determination and delight. Each evening let me look back on another day of complete obedience. At the end of my days, let there be the joy of looking back on a life that obeyed Your perfect will without the slightest hesitation and fulfilled Your purpose for me in my generation before I fell asleep. I ask this for Your pleasure and for the global advancement of Your righteous cause.

Amen.

A PRAYER FOR A GLIMPSE OF GOD'S GLORY

Prompted by Psalm 11:7

For the LORD is righteous, he loves justice; upright men will see his face.

Faithful Father. Merciful Master. Comforting Counselor.

I long for that first soul-satisfying moment when I shall see You face-to-face. I have every assurance that this moment-of-moments will be upon me when I pass through the valley of the shadow of death. Then I shall bid my final farewell to this body and stand immediately in Your presence. I also know that I shall see You when You return in glory to receive Your own. But if it pleases You, my Lord, let that moment come while still in this body. O that today would be the day! Whenever You choose that moment for me, I know that the joy of it will last forever. I shall never lose my wonder over the splendor of Your beauty.

Here on earth, I can become used to the most breathtaking scenes—majestic snowcapped mountains, a brilliant sunrise, a roaring waterfall, a bride in pure white. Not so with You, my Lord. What You are the moment I see You, You will always be. Your sheer beauty will never fade. Seeing Your beauty will fill a thousand eternities with never-ending awe and wonder. What wonderful anticipation! O that today would be the day!

No trial, no pain, no suffering or persecution for the sake of Your name can keep me from persevering till that moment of all moments has come. In the meantime, I ask every day for even a glimpse of Your glory. Open my eyes to see Your beauty in creation, in Your unsearchable ways, in Your perfect plans, and in the pleasure of being Your servant. Throughout this day fill my moments with a conscious sense of Your presence.

Amen.

A PRAYER FOR HEART-HUNGER AND SOUL-THIRST

Faithful Father, sovereign Shepherd, compassionate Counselor, triune God.

Create in me a heart-hunger that only You can satisfy. Stir in me a soul-thirst that only You can quench.

Yesterday You satisfied my hunger, but that was yesterday. Yesterday You quenched my thirst, but that was yesterday.

As I begin my communion with You this morning, grant me the gifts of a fresh heart-hunger and a renewed soul-thirst. Open my eyes to see Your beauty. Unstop my ears to hear Your voice. Shed light on my mind to understand Your Word, and touch my will to obey You with joy.

Amen.

A PRAYER FOR HUNGER AND THIRST FOR GOD

Prompted by Psalm 36:8

They feast on the abundance of your house; you give them drink from your river of delights.

Lord, what joy to discover that Your food and drink are both abundant and delightful! In the night I was awakened with the petition, "My Lord, place in my heart a hunger that only You can satisfy, and fill my soul with a thirst that only You can quench."

This morning You assured me that there is abundant food in Your house. Thank You for the open invitation to eat again and again and again. I can come to You morning-by-morning to be fed to the full. I can come for satisfying spiritual sustenance multiple times throughout the day. Let me come to You early every morning with an appetite that befits such abundance.

As for quenching my thirst, You offer a river of delights. My loving Lord, I come to You to fill my little cup. Let me drink from a full cup again and again and again. Yours is an endless supply of thirst-quenching, delightful drink.

Early this morning, my gracious God, I am filled with the joyful assurance that I shall never die of hunger or perish from thirst, for Your food is abundant and Your drink is a river of delights.

Amen.

A PRAYER TO HEAR THE VOICE OF GOD

Prompted by Psalm 83:1

O God, do not keep silent; be not quiet, O God, be not still.

My dear faithful Father, here I am again to meditate on Your Word. I view these Words in the Bible as Your very breath, as Your inspired and inerrant Words. Long after Your creation has been destroyed, Your eternal Word will remain. Neither its authority nor its power has diminished since Your Holy Spirit first inspired Your servants to write these words.

But, my loving Lord, I am not content just to read words; I must hear their message to me this very morning. I must sense their pulsating life, understand their clear instruction, delight in their eternal truth, and experience their transforming power.

O my Lord, energize all of my mental, emotional, and physical powers to hear, understand, and obey Your Word. Allow me to hear Your voice and see Your approving smile. Intensify my longing, desire, and appetite for Your Word. Let the good things You say to me silence all competing, conflicting voices.

I praise You that You are not silent or aloof. Thank You for allowing me to hear You this morning. My ears are cupped to hear Your voice speak throughout this day.

Amen.

A PRAYER OF THANKSGIVING FOR MY FATHER/SON RELATIONSHIP

Prompted by Mark 9:7

Then a cloud appeared and enveloped them, and a voice came from the cloud: "This is my Son, whom I love. Listen to him!"

Dear Father, I am not Your only begotten Son, but I am Your son, Your child. You have graciously given me the right and the power to be Your son. This is not a sonship handed down to me through Henry and Helen Sawatsky; neither is it a position I earned through some sacrificial or meritorious deed. This eternal sonship is the wonderful result of the new birth. It is a gracious gift of Your unmerited favor, Your undeserved mercy, and Your unfailing love.

Faithful Father, my entire being trembles with awe and with the deepest gratitude for such an intimate relationship with You. That You, almighty God, are my Father fills me with awe and worship. I fall to my knees in adoration; I place my hands over my mouth with wonder. I am stopped dead in my tracks over the thought of this intimate relationship with You. My tongue is still; it has no words but these:

"**I** am Your son forever."

"I **AM** Your son forever."

"I am **YOUR** son forever."

"I am Your **SON** forever."

"I am Your son **FOREVER**."

Praise be to God for this relationship of all relationships, a relationship that had a beginning on earth but will never end in heaven in Your holy presence.

Amen.

A PRAYER ABOUT THE PHARISEE IN ME

Prompted by Matthew 6:1

"Be careful not to do your 'acts of righteousness' before men, to be seen by them. If you do, you will have no reward from your Father in heaven."

My loving Lord, I detect the Pharisee in me. I confess to wanting others to think that I am holy, that I engage in acts of piety. I know better than to be as blatant as the Pharisees who made a public charade of their praying, fasting, and giving. Their motivation behind all they did was to earn the applause of man. How utterly repugnant! And yet I confess to secret enjoyment when others learn about my walk with You. Does this not make me a Pharisee? I embrace Your teaching that acts of piety are for Your eyes alone. I am determined to pray, fast, and give only for Your glory. In my heart I deprecate the phony practices of the Pharisees.

My Lord, I am content with having only You take note of my communion with You. May I never profess more with my mouth than I possess in my heart. Grant me the wisdom to strike a balance between living a transparent life before the members of my team and making a Pharisaical show of praying, fasting, and giving. Should anyone accidentally discover my secret acts of piety, let it be a surprise to them that the likes of me engages in holy practices.

My Lord, let it be Your recognition and Your reward that I seek. Let Your pleasure be my perpetual pursuit. Create in me a state of heart that cares nothing about man's applause. May Your glory alone be my quest.

Amen.

A PASSIONATE PRAYER FOR THE "OTHER SHEEP"

Prompted by John 17:20

"My prayer is not for them alone. I pray also for those who will believe in me through their message."

Sovereign Shepherd, in Your perfect foreknowledge, You have known before eternity past who will bow the knee to You in repentant, believing submission. You know whose hearts are being opened to embrace the Father's love.

Convicting Spirit of God, lead me to those You are drawing to my Savior. Let me be Your evangelist, one who takes advantage of every witnessing opportunity You orchestrate. Embolden me to speak freely and frequently as Jesus' witness.

Good Shepherd, grant me Your persistence to find the other sheep that are helplessly lost and cannot find their way into the safety of Your fold. Let me search for the other sheep until I find them.

As I intercede for the other sheep this morning, my heart is heavy for the Muslim world where so few, so very few have recognized You as the eternal Son of God. My heart yearns for them. Surely there are many Muslims among the other sheep. I implore You, sovereign Lord of the Harvest, to send harvesters into the Muslim world. Send them to Muslim homelands and to the millions of Muslim immigrants living among us in America and Europe.

Kindle in my soul fires of incessant intercession for the other sheep still groping about in spiritual darkness. I implore You to send "under shepherds" to bring the other sheep to You.

Amen.

A PRAYER FOR BOLDNESS
IN EVANGELISM

Prompted by Psalm 105:1

Give thanks to the Lord, call on his name; make known among the nations what he has done.

Almighty God, I join the songwriter in his petition that the nations come to know You and Your marvelous deeds. The peoples of this world are blind to Your wonderful works of creation. Their understanding of You is distorted; their blind eyes cannot see Your beauty, nor can their deaf ears hear Your voice. They attribute Your handiwork in creation to random, chance happenings spread over millions of years.

O my Lord, reveal Your glory, Your majesty, and Your might. I long for the day when Your glory will cover the earth as the waters cover the sea. Send Your messengers everywhere to proclaim the Lord. I have devoted my life to the most noble of causes—the global proclamation of the good news of Your Son's substitutionary death, burial, and resurrection. I have come to see my mission as an urgent, global, rescue operation. Intensify my passion for the lost. Stir in me a boldness to identify myself openly with You, my Lord. Let me be Your fearless, fruitful evangelist. Use me to ignite fires in the souls of others so that they too will be engaged in relentless, aggressive, and culturally sensitive evangelism.

Amen.

SECTION III

Intimacy with God:
Topical Essays

INTIMACY WITH GOD AND THE GREAT COMMANDMENT

"The most important [commandment,]" answered Jesus, "is this: 'Hear, O Israel, the Lord our God, the Lord is one. Love the Lord your God with all your heart and with all your soul and with all your mind and with all your strength.' The second is this: 'Love your neighbor as yourself.' There is no greater commandment than these." (Mark 12:29-31)

The sovereign Lord of the harvest has called many of us to devote a lifetime to cross-cultural missionary service. Understandably, we have come to view the Great Commission as much of our motivation for the global missionary enterprise. The Great Commission has become our missionary manifesto. We preach, teach, and meditate on the five versions of the Great Commission, one in each of the four Gospels and a final one just prior to Jesus' ascension as recorded in the Acts of the Apostles. Jesus personally gave all five Great Commission statements to His church and to its leaders.

I have personally referred to the Great Commission as the *grand goal of the church* and as our *permanent marching orders* from the Captain of our salvation. I have also pointed out that the Great Commission in the New Testament is deeply rooted in God's Old Testament promise to Abraham to bless all peoples through him. I have exhorted my audiences in local churches to make *Christ's last command our first concern*.

Our first concern? Actually, there is a command in both the Old and New Testaments that trumps all other commands simply because it is the first and greatest commandment. This means that we must give this command a place ahead of all other commands—yes, even before the Great Commission. In Matthew's gospel, Jesus Himself called this the greatest commandment, and in Mark's account of the same incident, He called it the most important commandment. Not only is the Great Commandment to love God with our entire being the greatest and the most important of all commandments, it serves as a summary of the whole Bible. Think of it! This command is so comprehensive and so far reaching in its application that to obey it means to obey all other commands.

Before examining the Great Commandment more closely, we must note that in the Gospels only Mark's account includes the confession of faith recited by all devout Jews: *"Hear O Israel, the Lord our God, the Lord is one."* Two times daily, all Jews reminded one another that there is no God beside their sovereign Lord; and furthermore, this one true God has established a loving covenant relationship with them. The unity of God and His covenant of love with His people form the basis for God's command to love Him supremely. The love we are commanded to render to God is not a one-sided directive. Before He commanded us to love Him with the whole heart, soul, mind, and strength, He demonstrated His unfailing love toward us.

> The love we are commanded to render to God is not a one-sided directive.

What is the significance of love for God with heart, soul, mind, and strength? These four categories are conduits through which we convey our love to God. They are channels that transmit our deepest affection toward the triune God. Although we must exercise care not to distinguish these four categories too sharply, since the Scriptures list them individually and consecutively, we are justified in making some degree of distinction. We could liken them to four "tributaries" flowing into one broadening stream of passionate love and affection for almighty God. These four parts represent the unique capacities of each child of God. They are the totality of all our faculties. Obedience to the Great Commandment requires that we summon our whole being to love our God supremely, wholeheartedly, uniquely, and exclusively.

My *heart* is the wellspring of my deepest affection. This affection must be reserved exclusively for God. There can be no rival. My *soul* represents my very life. Every breath I draw, including my final one, must pulsate with love for God. Beginning in our youth and continuing into old age, we must see to it that the capacity of our hearts to love God grows continually. My *mind* is the repository of all of my intellectual powers, my knowledge, my wisdom, and my education. Every creative idea and all insights into eternal truth, all of my training and experience must reflect passion for the one true God and His wonderful ways. My *strength* symbolizes my health, energy, and capacity for labor. All sacrificial acts of service must be offerings of devoted love to my faithful Father.

The Great Commandment requires that the *whole* heart, soul, mind, and strength must be consecrated to loving God. Even the slightest reserve is unacceptable and falls short of a love for God that is complete. There must be wholehearted, exuberant, and joyous love for God. In His post-resurrection conversation with Peter, Jesus could have asked, "Peter, after denying Me three times, have you finally come to terms with your human frailties? Do you agree that you've been overly self-confident? Can I count on you not to deny Me again?" Peter may have expected similar stinging queries, but Jesus had more important questions to ask of him. Instead of a conversation that focused on Peter's denial, He gently asked him three probing questions: *"Simon son of John, do you truly love me more than these?"*. . . *"Simon son of John, do you truly love me?"*. . . *"Simon son of John, do you love me?"* (John 21:15-17).

This personal exchange between Jesus and Peter beautifully illustrates obedience to the Great Commandment. Jesus wanted Peter's love *before* his service. Furthermore, He wanted Peter's love *more* than his service. In essence Jesus said, "Peter, *love* me, *follow* me, *serve* me!" in that order. Before Jesus commissioned Peter for public service, He asked Peter to take private inventory of his love for God. Before we circle the globe in obedience to the Great Commission to preach the gospel to everyone everywhere, we do well to allow Jesus to probe our obedience to the Great Commandment.

Love for God must precede service for God. Labor for God must be the overflow of love for God. Whenever we reverse the order, all of our ministry, including our work for God, becomes a dutiful task. The order in the Great Commandment is love for God before labor for God, allegiance to God before an assignment from God, intimacy with God before service for God.

Jesus made the conversation with Peter very personal. There was no mistaking whom Jesus meant when he addressed Peter three times as "Simon son of John." It is apparent that Jesus was probing Peter's motivation for wanting to serve Him.

In a variety of ways, Jesus asks personal penetrating questions of us. Why, for example, do I get up before dawn to read the Scriptures and pray? Is it because I have heard that other great men and women of God do so, or is this motivated out of a heart hunger and a soul thirst for the living God? Why do I engage in evangelism? Is it because I have been exhorted to the point of guilt if I do not, or do I tell others about Jesus Christ because I love Him deeply? Why is it that I am a missionary church planter? Is it because I have been told that this is the most strategic method of fulfilling the Great Commission, or is it because I love Jesus Christ the Architect and Builder of His church?

Nearing the end of his conversation with Jesus, Peter was momentarily distracted when he glanced at John. "What about him?" Peter asked.

Jesus did not discuss His plans for John with Peter. Peter was simply to follow Jesus. Just as we have an "audience of One" in the God we love, follow, and serve, God also has an "audience of one" in the way He deals with each of us. The markers He has set for our

> God's path is not a freeway where the masses walk.

path are uniquely ours. God's path is not a freeway where the masses walk; it is a clearly marked personal path on which to follow Jesus.

How difficult it is to listen to all of the voices that exhort us, and how impossible to please everyone who has a well-intentioned plan for us. The Great Commandment makes crystal clear that God is our "audience of one" to love supremely. Our primary task all our days is to develop a lifelong love relationship with the Father, Son, and Holy Spirit. Loving Him supremely, following Him closely, and serving Him exuberantly will enhance our quest for intimacy with God.

Jesus linked the Great Commandment to the second greatest commandment, which is to love our neighbor as ourselves. In summary, these two commands call for a passion for God and compassion for our needy neighbor. There are in these two commandments both the Godward and the manward dimensions. The picture is not complete until we love our neighbor as ourselves. Since Jesus linked the two commandments, we must do the same. We demonstrate our love for God by our acts of compassion for man. We must not, indeed cannot, separate these two commands. The second flows out of the first. True love for man is contingent on wholehearted love for God. We may be able to muster pity and even empathy for the plight of unfortunate people, but compassion for my neighbor in need is possible only as an overflow of a love relationship with almighty God.

INTIMACY WITH GOD AND "OUR FIRST LOVE"

A prized stamp in my American passport is dated August 28, 1996. It simply says "Patmos, Greece." When Muriel and I arrived on Patmos by ship, we had just come off a tour of the seven Christian church sites in Anatolia, Turkey. We read the appropriate letter at the ruins of each of the seven churches, letters written from Patmos, a tiny six- by ten-mile arid island. Our twenty-four-hour visit to Patmos turned out to be the capstone to our travels.

The apostle John was banished to Patmos by the emperor Domitian *"because of the word of God and the testimony of Jesus"* (Revelation 1:9). It was on the Lord's Day while at worship that John was given not only the letters to the seven churches, but also the last book in our Bible, the Revelation of Jesus Christ (see Revelation 1:9-11).

Our focus in this essay on intimacy with God is Jesus' letter to the Ephesian Church (see Revelation 2:1-7). The church at Ephesus had a very colorful history. She had the distinction of more than two years of teaching from none other than the apostle Paul (Acts 19:8-10). Apollos the apologist also ministered to the believers at Ephesus (Acts 18:24-26). The Ephesian church was given wide coverage in the New Testament Scriptures, including Paul's epistle to the Ephesians and the letter from Jesus Christ, the risen, ascended Lord in the Book of Revelation.

The church at Ephesus was born in the midst of fierce opposition from the Jews, from the seven sons of Sceva who tried to counterfeit Paul's demonstrations of power, and from citywide riots stirred up by Demetrius, a silversmith who feared a loss in business from the sale of the goddess Artemis' images. This church witnessed dramatic conversions to Christ, for there were many who publicly burned their costly occult paraphernalia (see Acts 19:17-20). Now, roughly forty-five years after the church at Ephesus had been planted by Paul and his team, it received a letter from Jesus Christ, the Head of the Church, and from the Holy Spirit who also spoke powerfully to each of the churches.

In His letter to the Ephesian Church, Jesus included both words of commendation and condemnation. He introduced Himself as the one who holds the leaders of the seven churches in His right hand, as well as the one who is walking among the churches (see Revelation 2:1).

Jesus' list of commendations is impressive. He knew all about the Ephesians' hard work, their uncompromising stand against evil and heretical men, their endurance in the face of hardship for the cause of Christ, and their hatred for the same things Jesus hated. Who among us would not covet such a résumé of achievements? What pastor would not be elated with this assessment, especially since it came from Jesus? This is a grand slam, an A-plus! Here we have a list of twenty-first century evangelical values, the "Grammy Awards" for best work ethic, best antiheresy program, and best endurance test.

Today, any church with such an endorsement from Jesus would be featured frequently in our leading Christian journals. Its pastor would travel the world putting on seminars and hawking his "how to" books and videos. With a report card like this, Ephesus would qualify as one of the top ten evangelical churches in America.

But there is more. There is also a word *of condemnation.*

The applause and the high fives almost drown Jesus' single weighty word of warning. It takes time for Jesus' indictment to penetrate the euphoria over the first half of His good report card. As the force of Jesus' condemnation sinks in, it sounds like a series of exploding thunderclaps from a blue sky. Finally, there is silence. He has our attention. What is Jesus saying? There is more in His letter? Jesus is now saying that He has one thing against the church at Ephesus. And what might that be? What really matters after all the good things Jesus has already said? Surely the five A-pluses would overshadow one lower grade. The grade point average would still be high. Why not focus on the multiple strengths rather than on one lone weakness?

Jesus is saying that the church at Ephesus had fallen from its *first love.* He went on to say that apart from a return to *her first love,* her

> Apart from a return to her first love, her light would be extinguished.

light would be extinguished. It was that serious. Suddenly, it was like discovering terminal cancer right after winning ten million dollars. Ephesus's very survival as a church now took on front-burner urgency.

We must linger longer over Jesus' condemnation, for what He saw in the Ephesians He may well see in us too. Consider these translations of Jesus' indicting words: *"You walked away from* your first love" (MSG, emphasis added); *"You don't love me as at first"* (TLB); "You have abandoned the love you had at first" (RSV); *"You have less love now than you used to"* (JB).

This is the language of a wounded friend, the words of a spouse whose partner has become distant, or the cry of one in anguish over a warm friendship relationship turned cold. Like graying hair, the change had been gradual. The believers at Ephesus were quite oblivious to what had happened. They thought they were doing very well. Jesus' evaluation seemed to confirm this. Neither the Ephesians themselves nor those looking into this community of Christians from the outside observed what Jesus saw. Only the One whose *"eyes were like blazing* fire" (Revelation 1:14) saw their fatal flaw. Only the living Lord walking among His churches could see this serious slippage in *their first love.* Nothing, not even the hidden sins of the heart, escapes His scrutiny. Little-by-little their earlier fervor and passion had waned.

Ephesus had become a larger church with a broader reputation, but tragically, it had also become a smaller church with a shriveling *first love.* They had not ceased to love Jesus, but now they loved Him less. Their hearts were no longer completely committed toward Jesus. Although their programs continued apace, the former fires of a white-hot love relationship with Jesus were now but a flicker. Even their commitment to evangelical doctrines remained strong, but these became brittle and mechanical because their love for Jesus Christ no longer energized their beliefs. This was why Jesus sounded the alarm. He is calling the believers at Ephesus back to their former love relationship with Himself.

What did Jesus mean by *first love?* Reflecting on *the first love* of newlyweds or *the first love* of a newborn child of God, we might characterize *first love* as affection which is fresh, simple, pure, unselfish, fervent, passionate, and tender. *First love* is delighting in Jesus' presence, longing to hear His voice, feeding hungrily on His Word, communing with Him as with

> First love is an intimate love relationship with Jesus Christ.

the most intimate friend, eagerness for His approval, trusting Him completely, obeying Him immediately, and talking about Him freely and frequently. *First love* maintains the freshness, the excitement of a perpetual beginning. Time has no power to *alter first love;* it never turns stale or feeble with age. *First love* is the believer's fountain of youth. In short, *first love* is an intimate love relationship with Jesus Christ; it is intimacy with the Almighty.

Jesus attaches much greater importance to our love relationship *with* Him than to our service *for* Him. Didn't Jesus value their hard work, their orthodoxy, and their steadfastness? Of course He did, but He longs that all we do for Him flows out of our love for Him. Jesus' post-resurrection conversation with Peter powerfully illustrates His longing for our love. Jesus did not ask Peter if he had learned his lesson or if he had developed a coping strategy to face future temptation. Instead, He asked Peter three times if he loved Him (see John 21:15ff). In essence, Jesus was saying to Peter, "Your service for Me must flow out of your affection for Me." That is *the first love* Jesus desires.

First love is also vividly defined by Mary's extravagant act of devotion to Jesus. Judas hypocritically criticized her for pouring ointment worth a whole year's wages onto Jesus' feet and wiping them with her hair (see John 12:3ff). Jesus defended her loving act of devotion as the *first love* He desires. Elsewhere, the same Mary chose to sit at Jesus' feet to listen to His teaching rather than scurry about the house doing domestic chores. She could take care of these later. Jesus commended her for choosing what *a first love* would choose (see Luke 10:38ff).

First love is rarely abandoned for sinful substitutes. It is lost through neglect, carelessness, and lapses in personal discipline. *First love* is lost through thinking that yesterday's fires will provide today's warmth, through forgetting that we do not naturally set either our hearts or our minds on things above, and through buying into the mistaken notion that our service for God is more important than our affection for God.

Refusal to resolve a conflict with a brother or sister may actually be the leading cause for inching away from a love relationship with Jesus Christ. In a relationship it's possible to tell a lie and even to live a lie pretending that all is well, but it's impossible to come before God to pray a lie (see Matthew 5:23-24).

What counsel did Jesus give the Christians at Ephesus? How could they recover their *"first love?"* First, Jesus said, you must *"remember the height from which you have fallen"* (Revelation 2:5). Go back in time! Reconstruct the most intimate moments with Jesus Christ and compare them with your present level of love for Him. Such intimate moments with the Master are not meant to be occasional but continual. My love relationship with Jesus Christ is like a fire that must be stoked and tended. Fires not supplied with wood go out and become a pile of cold, gray ashes. The fuel of continual communion, devotion, obedience, and confession can keep my love for Jesus hot. Even one day of neglect is serious. Is there a more important task, a more satisfying occupation than to heap "fuel" onto the fire of my love relationship with Jesus Christ?

Second, you must "repent." Coldness, indifference, distance, apathy, and messed-up priorities are all dangerous, deadening sins. Turn away from them! Confess them to God! Allow your heart to be broken! Let the tears of remorse flow! Rid yourself of the things that usurped the preeminence Jesus must have! Rearrange your life to make ample room for a fervent love relationship with Jesus.

Third, Jesus commanded, "Do the things you did at first" or "repeat what you used to do before the fall." Retrace your steps! Go back! Do again what you used to do to fan your love for God into white-hot flames. They were simple, childlike acts of devotion, unhurried times of prayer, conversations with God about everything. Going back will take time, but remember, wandering away from your *first love* happened gradually or unconsciously over time. The return journey cannot be made in a moment.

Remember! Repent! Repeat! If you or I have strayed even a short distance from a passionate love relationship with our Savior, like the prodigal son, let's come to our senses and retrace our steps back to our *first love* for Jesus Christ.

INTIMACY WITH GOD AND ABIDING IN CHRIST

Halfway through the Upper Room discourse, Jesus shared some timeless lessons on intimacy with God and fruit bearing. He had just shared the Passover meal with His disciples and immediately thereafter astounded them by insisting on washing their feet. To honor a much-loved teacher, occasionally pupils would wash his feet, but never, ever would the teacher stoop to wash the feet of his students.

Judas had just been identified as the traitor, and subsequently missed hearing Jesus' promise of a personally-prepared heavenly home, as well as Jesus' promise of the comforting Counselor who would remain with His followers when He returned to the Father. Judas also missed hearing Jesus' teaching about abiding in Him and fruit-bearing. This teaching was reserved for Jesus' friends.

The fruit Jesus speaks of in John 15 is a godly life or a Christlike character. Paul called it *"the fruit of the Spirit"* (Galatians 5:22-23). This fruit can also appropriately be viewed as the very character of Christ or as qualities of Christlikeness. What could possibly be more attractive to the world than progressively more of Jesus' love, joy, peace, patience, kindness, goodness, faithfulness, gentleness, and self-control borne through by the Holy Spirit? Could anything be more appealing than a life that becomes progressively more like Jesus?

The three "players" in Jesus' parable are the *vine,* the *branches,* and the *gardener.* Jesus Himself is the vine, we are the branches, and the Father is the Gardener. A gardener's deepest desire is for more and more fruit. For this reason he nurtures, waters, protects, prunes, and labors endlessly over the vines in his vineyard. An abundant harvest of fruit is the gardener's chief delight. Where he sees fruit, he prunes so that the branch *"will be even more fruitful"* (John 15:2).

Our Father does the same with us. In our case He allows afflictions, tests, trials, and difficulties to do the pruning, but always under His watchful eye and skillful hand. The objective is more fruit, i.e., more Christlikeness, deeper holiness, and more intimate communion with the Father. We honor and exalt God when we *"bear much fruit"* (John 15:8). He becomes heaven's glad Gardener when He sees us transformed into the likeness of His Son.

Jesus teaches us several basic lessons about fruit bearing. First, when He speaks of "fruit," "more fruit," and "much fruit," it is clear that He desires our fruit bearing to be *progressively more abundant*, i.e., steadily more fruit both in quantity and quality. Second, our fruit is *predetermined*, i.e., Jesus has appointed us to bear certain fruits that will fulfill His purpose for us (see John 15:16). Third, the fruit borne by Jesus' followers is *permanent*, i.e., not perishable but lasting. To sum up, as we remain (abide) in Christ, we will bear more and more fruit, we will bear the fruit Jesus intends, and, we will bear fruit that is imperishable.

> As we remain (abide) in Christ, we will bear more and more fruit.

Another important lesson is this: apart from remaining (abiding, continuing, dwelling) in Christ there can be no fruit. It is not our education, our personality, our clever strategies, our resources, or our natural abilities that produce fruit. The fruit of Christlikeness is exclusively the result of abiding in Christ.

This brings us to the need of attempting a description of abiding in Christ. Consider the following suggestions as to the meaning of abiding in Christ:

- to stay put and not to stray from Him
- to remain near to Jesus and not flit about hither and yon
- to cling steadfastly to Christ
- to remain in intimate communion with Jesus
- to rest or relax in my union with Christ
- to allow the life and power of Christ to flow through me
- to be totally devoted to Jesus
- to do whatever it takes to cultivate the most intimate relationship with Jesus Christ
- to welcome the pruning process as necessary for greater fruitfulness
- to submit myself joyfully and completely to the lordship of Jesus Christ
- to choose Him as my closest Companion and my dearest Friend
- to allow His teachings to instruct and direct me.

This, in part, is what is meant by abiding in Christ.

Ten times in the first eleven verses of John 15, Jesus speaks of abiding in Him. Several times He speaks in the imperative. Clearly, remaining in Christ is more than a suggestion. Abiding in Christ must be understood as one of His commands. If there is to be the fruit of Christlikeness, there is no alternative but to obey His command to abide in Him.

> He has singled us out to have the closest of relationships with Him.

We must not think for one moment that remaining in Christ is a one-sided relationship. Not at all! In this intimate relationship, we need not overcome reluctance on Jesus part. At every turn He has taken the initiative. He has singled us out to have the closest of relationships with Him. Jesus promised His eleven disciples in the Upper Room, *"I will remain in you"* (John 15:4).

Jesus is not speaking here to pagans but to His devoted followers who have their names recorded in the Lamb's Book of Life, who have received the free gift of eternal life, who have repented before God and exercised faith in the finished work of Christ. Positionally, they are all in Christ. There is not only communication and communion with God, there is also union with Him. But when it comes to Christlikeness, to influence in the kingdom, to a passionate pursuit of intimacy with God, to joy, or to Christian maturity, not all Christians are the same. The difference is in the degree to which the "abiding in Christ" relationship is being cultivated.

Although Jesus likens us to fruit-bearing branches, there is one major difference between us and the branches. We have a will that is willfully wayward; the branches do not. Jesus' command to remain in Him means that it will be obeyed or disobeyed, heard or ignored. This is a choice we must make. We do not automatically bear the fruit of Christlikeness. Such fruit is borne only through an intimate relationship with our Savior.

In addition to the analogy of the vine and the branches, Jesus goes on to describe the intimacy He wants with us by describing the relationship He has with His Father. In other words, Jesus' intimacy with the Father is what our intimacy with the Son should look like. Jesus tells the eleven in the Upper Room that the Father's

> We show our love by obeying Jesus' commands.

love for Him is the love He has for them. This, Jesus says, is precisely the love we are to remain in (see John 15:9). How is that love demonstrated? By obedience! Just as Jesus expressed His love to the Father by total obedience to Him, we show our love by obeying Jesus' commands.

It is not surprising that prayer becomes an integral part of the abiding life. It is the combination of remaining in Jesus and allowing

His teachings to remain in us which opens wide the door to asking and receiving whatever we wish. On the surface, this promise seems somewhat reckless. Could it possibly be true? Surely the fine print will reveal that there's a catch. Isn't it a risk for Jesus to hold out such a promise? Remember, receiving whatever we wish is contingent on remaining in Jesus and in His teachings. The truth is that an intimate relationship with Jesus coupled with knowledge and submission to His teaching will so instruct our asking and so bring it into alignment with His desires, that all questions about answered prayer are removed. Later, the condition of asking in Jesus' name is added (see John 15:16).

Using Jesus' name in prayer represents His endorsement, His agreement with our request. How else can we know what He endorses apart from an intimate relationship with Him and familiarity with His teachings?

My dear brothers and sisters, please join me in going deeper into a life of abiding in Christ. How much greater the impact on a lost world such a life would make! How infinitely more attractive is each act of service when it proceeds from the life of a worker bearing the abundant fruit of Christlikeness.

INTIMACY WITH GOD AND CONFESSION

Have mercy on me, O God, according to your unfailing love; according to your great compassion blot out my transgressions. Wash away all of my iniquity and cleanse me from my sin. (Psalm 51:1-2)

If we confess our sins, he is faithful and just and will forgive us our sins and purify us from all unrighteousness. (1 John 1:9)

The seven most difficult words in the English language are "I was wrong; will you forgive me?"

Pride resists making so stark a confession. Pride pleads for a lighter sentence; it holds out hope for an acquittal without a confession of guilt. If a confession must be made at all, pride is very creative in coming up with less painful versions such as: "I was wrong but so were you." "I concede that was a dumb thing to do, but you provoked me to do it." "That was silly of me; whatever was I thinking?" "It was just an unintended slip of the tongue or a temporary lapse of my sensibilities." "This really made me look bad. But you and I both know that this wasn't really me." These are watered-down, anemic versions of a true confession of wrongdoing.

If the offense was anger, nagging, or lying, it's not enough to call it silly, dumb, or a slip of the tongue. It was an offense and must be treated head-on as such. To draw attention to someone else's wrong or to blame others for making me do what I did will not rid me of the offense. The only course of action that will dislodge an offense is a candid, contrite confession.

For a relationship between two estranged parties to be restored, two things must happen. First, the offender must ask forgiveness of the offended, and second, the offended must extend forgiveness. Apart from seeking and granting forgiveness, the circle of reconciliation remains broken. Depending on the nature of the offense, the forgiveness may or may not be instantaneous. It is one thing to say the words, "I forgive you," and quite another to actually extend complete, unqualified, unconditional forgiveness. It may take some time for the pain to subside, but a genuine confession is the key to making complete healing possible. The offended person must remember that sooner or later he/she too will need to ask forgiveness. Who among us does not need daily forgiveness from our fellow heaven-bound pilgrims?

> To deal with a sin we must do so from God's perspective as well as from man's.

All sin is first and foremost against God (see Psalm 51:4), but invariably it is also against a spouse, a family member, a ministry colleague, a friend, or a church. To deal with a sin, we must do so from God's perspective as well as from man's. Before the relationship with God and with man can be restored, there must be a contrite confession of a specific sin coupled with a humble plea for forgiveness. As long as there is a refusal to come clean with confession coupled with a sincere request for forgiveness, the break in fellowship with God and man will continue. Deal with an offense quickly before it hardens like setting concrete. Old, deeply entrenched offenses are much harder to deal with.

David stood "naked" before God as he made his painful confession to Him. Who among us has not felt both the pathos and the hope in David's Godward plea for forgiveness? He based his appeal for God's undeserved mercy on His unfailing love and great compassion. On numerous other occasions he had counted on God's loving kindness; he could do so again. He did not argue with God; he agreed totally with God's "guilty" verdict. He made neither excuses nor attempts to shift the blame to someone else. He did not say that he had fallen victim to some unfortunate chain of circumstances. David did not characterize what he had done as a sudden, unavoidable slip or as a stupid mistake. He owned up to *his* transgression, *his* iniquity, and *his* sin. He had transgressed; that is, blatantly disobeyed by crossing over the line drawn by a holy God. He acknowledged his propensity toward sin. He came to see his sin as an act of defiance against the God who loved him.

Do we think it strange that David directed so much of his confession of sin toward God and not more to his outrageous offense against Uriah and Bathsheba? He did indeed write more about offending almighty God. We may think David's emphasis unusual because we tend to find our confession to man most difficult. What could be the reason for this? Is it because we have failed to see how pure and holy God is and at the same time how heinous sin is? I believe this to be the case.

We must come to see all sin from God's perspective. We must understand that the sole reason for the death of Jesus on the cross was our sin. To offend someone is a serious matter, but to offend our holy God is infinitely more serious. This does not mean that confession of our sin against those we offend is unnecessary, but it does mean that the sincerity and contrition of our confession to man must flow out of brokenness before God. Only as we see our sin from God's perspective will we be capable of making an adequate confession of wrong-doing to man.

> We must come to see all sin from God's perspective.

Isaiah was given a vision of God's holiness (see Isaiah 6:1-3). Immediately he also saw his own sinfulness. The closer and more intimate our walk with God, the blacker and more ugly sin becomes to us. Failure to see our sin from a brother or sister's perspective usually means that we are minimizing its gravity. We will no doubt need help to understand, feel, and see our sin from another's perspective. We can pray to God to open our eyes to the pain we have caused. We can ask the person we offended to help us with his/her perspective.

Only as we come to feel some of the pain caused by our words, actions, or neglect will we be able to make an acceptable confession. Apart from such an understanding, our confession will come across as shallow and even hollow. Demonstrating by the choice of words in our confession that we have understood the perspective of the offended person will help to authenticate it as real. A half-hearted or general apology may only make matters worse. If we value the forgiveness we are seeking, it will be worth considerable effort to prepare our confession carefully. This means that the words which frame our confession must flow from a broken heart. There cannot be even a hint of self-justification. But, we ask, what about the other person? I too was offended. The other person's confession is not my responsibility. The same Holy Spirit at work in *my* heart is also bringing about conviction in the one who offended you. You can count on it!

What does confession of sin have to do with intimacy with God? Unconfessed and consequently unforgiven sin becomes a barrier between us and God. Unconfessed sin robs us of enjoying the presence of God, puts a dark cloud in the sky of our relationship with Him, and throws us off balance in our ability to function with confidence. When we confess our sin to God, we discover again what a precious treasure a clear conscience is. I say it again, there is no other solution to ridding us of an offense but to retrace our steps, return to the one offended, own up to our sin, and humbly ask for forgiveness. A refusal to confess our sin is prolonging an argument with God; it is a refusal to align ourselves with God's guilty verdict. I speak from experience; this is a struggle we can never win. God's judgment is correct, and we must agree with it. The sooner we accept God's guilty verdict, the sooner we can be restored to an intimate, enjoyable relationship with Him.

INTIMACY WITH GOD AND A BROKEN HEART

The Lord is close to the brokenhearted and saves those who are crushed in spirit. (Psalm 34:18)

The sacrifices of God are a broken spirit; a broken and contrite heart, O God, you will not despise. (Psalm 51:17)

King David's colorful life brings to mind several biblical scenes— killing the nine-foot-tall, blasphemous, braggart Goliath with a slingshot; being secretly anointed as king of Israel by Samuel while still a shepherd boy; playing the harp to soothe King Saul's troubled mind; bonding with Jonathan into the deepest man-to-man friendship; fleeing as a fugitive from Saul; ascending the throne for a forty-year reign over Israel; and writing hymns and prayers of worship to the God he loved supremely. That's David!

God loved David. He handpicked him to lead His people as a shepherd leads his sheep. God said of David. *"He's a man whose heart beats to my heart, a man who will do what I tell him"* (Acts 13:22 MSG). God promised David greatness. He also promised David that the Messiah would be one of his descendants. After David died, his character, his conduct, and his devotion to God became the litmus test for all of his successors; either they measured up to the Davidic standard or they fell short of it.

However, there is one more scene in David's life as familiar as the felling of Goliath. It is not a "skeleton" hidden away in some closet, for you and everyone else knows it well. It is not a pretty chapter. I am referring, of course, to David's adultery with Bathsheba, his murder of Bathsheba's husband Uriah, and his unsuccessful attempt to cover up his sin.

God did love David, but not with a permissive love that looks the other way and lets even His chosen leader off with a light slap on the hand. First, God took David through a time of the most excruciating repentance. Next, God sent faithful Nathan to bring news of God's judgment on David and his household: *"The sword will never depart from your house, because you despised me and took the wife of Uriah the Hittite to be your own . . . Out of your own household I am going to bring calamity upon you"* (2 Samuel 12:10-11).

Did God forgive David? Yes, mercifully He did! Did he deserve to be forgiven? No! Forgiveness was granted only by God's grace and mercy. Could he continue as King? Yes, undeservedly he could. Did he reap what he sowed? Yes, indeed! Did his sin affect his family? Tragically, yes, as we shall see. The consequences to his family were so horrendous that David never again enjoyed the carefree peace and tranquility that had characterized his life to this point.

At some time during Bathsheba's pregnancy, the realization of what David had done broke his heart. David's words of repentance in two separate Psalms drip with heart-rending remorse. Eugene Peterson's paraphrase in *The Message* captures David's wretchedness and contrition in these graphic words from two Psalms: *"When I kept it all inside, my bones turned to powder, my words became daylong groans. The pressure never let up; the juices of my life dried up. Then I let it all out; I said. 'I'll make a clean breast of my failures to God.' Suddenly the pressure was gone—my guilt dissolved, my sin disappeared"* (Psalm 32:3-5 MSG).

"Generous in love—God give grace! Huge in mercy—wipe out my bad record. Scrub away my guilt, soak out my sins in your laundry. I know how bad I've been; my sins are staring me down. You're the One I've violated, and you've seen it all, seen the full extent of my evil. You have all the facts before you; whatever you decide about me is fair. I've been out of step with you for a long time, in the wrong since before I was born. What you're after is truth from the inside out. Enter me, then; conceive a new, true life" (Psalm 51:1-6 MSG).

Had David insisted on rationalizing or justifying himself, his communion with God would have been permanently impaired. There could have been no further delight in the presence of God. His sin would have become a wall, a high wall between him and God. He could not enjoy his salvation. Thankfully, however, his repentance was genuine; God's forgiveness was complete—so complete that David wrote about the happiness that comes from having every sin in his account with God blotted out (see Psalm 32:1). David has much to teach us about brokenheartedness. His own heart was shattered over his sin against the God he loved.

Even though there was forgiveness and restoration to fellowship with God, there were still some painful consequences to his sin. There always are. Tragedy struck his household repeatedly:

- David's son Ammon raped his sister Tamar.
- David's son Absalom killed his brother Ammon as revenge for raping his sister Tamar.
- Absalom conspired to steal the throne from his father David and was killed in the process.
- David's son Adonijah tried to take the throne by force and was also killed in the process.

What a painful list of consequences! All for a moment of ecstasy with Bathsheba! Let us never underestimate the havoc sin can create for us.

Further, let us never underestimate the long road back to restore intimacy with God.

David has much to teach us about brokenheartedness. His own heart was shattered over his sin against the God he loved. He felt utterly crushed over the

> David has much to teach us about broken-heartedness.

consequences of his grievous sin against his own immediate family. Many are the times he must have sighed, "If only . . ." "If only I had not allowed myself to be in a position of being tempted." "If only I had not thought 'Lesser kings do as they please, why can't I?'" "If only I had not thought foolishly that I could fabricate a permanent cover-up." The pain of David's brokenness was so severe that it should serve as a big red light for all time saying, "Stop! Danger! Slippery slope ahead! Don't go this way! Run!"

David learned that God took absolutely no delight in religious ritual while David was harboring unconfessed sin in his heart. Apparently he continued temple sacrifices without interruption. He tried to satisfy God by offering sacrifices, but God turned His eyes away from his offerings on the altar and looked directly into his heart. David discovered that what God really wanted from him was the sacrifice of a repentant and broken heart. When he came to God with confession, brokenness, and contrition, God received him.

So then, what does brokenness have to do with intimacy with God? Or more precisely, what does brokenness have to do with the restoration of a lost intimacy with

> A broken heart puts us back onto God's wavelength.

God? A broken heart puts us back onto God's wavelength. The opposite of brokenness is a heart that is defiant, proud, unyielding, and self-justifying. God will hold such a heart at arm's length. Such a frame of heart is repugnant to God. On the other hand, a repentant sorrow, a genuine grief, a weeping heart, an honest confession—these are the attitudes with which we must approach God. When we do, we are in alignment with our faithful Father's holiness. When we do, we agree with God's verdict. When we do, we accept His terms. When we do, intimacy with the Almighty is restored. God assures us that He does not despise or belittle a broken heart.

David suffered severely over the loss of intimate communion with God. He pleaded with God to restore the joy of his salvation. Having his sin exposed before an entire nation was painful, but the thought of remaining distant from God was infinitely more painful.

Whether before or after his restoration to an intimate walk with God we do not know, but David adds to his understanding of brokenness with these words: *"The LORD is close to the brokenhearted and saves those who are crushed in spirit"* (Psalm 34:18). Think of it. The Lord is near to the brokenhearted. He has an especially intimate relationship with those whose hearts are crushed. God takes particular notice of those whose hearts are humble and contrite and draws near to them. One of God's requirements is that we walk humbly with Him (Micah 6:8).

Consider this as a final thought, directly from Scripture, on brokenness: *"This is what the LORD says: Heaven is my throne, and the earth is my footstool. Where is the house you will build for me? Where will my resting place be? Has not my hand made all these things, and so they came into being? declares the LORD. This is the one I esteem: he who is humble and contrite in spirit, and trembles at my word"* (Isaiah 66:1-2).

INTIMACY WITH GOD AND HEART HUNGER

In the Bible's hymnbook, I discover an intense heart-hunger for God, a hunger that at times rises to ravenous proportions. The hymn writers' pursuit was not primarily for the benefits which come from God's generous hand. No, it was God Himself they longed for. They craved the presence of God, desired to hear His voice, and longed to see His face. Here is a small sampling of their heart-hunger pangs for God and of their expressions of ecstatic joy over sensing His presence:

> "You will fill me with joy in your presence, with eternal pleasures at your right hand." (Psalm 16:11, emphasis added)

> "One thing I ask of the Lord, this is what I seek: that I may dwell in the house of the Lord all the days of my life, to gaze upon the beauty of the Lord and to seek him in his temple." (Psalm 27:4, emphasis added)

> "They feast on the abundance of your house; you give them drink from your river of delights." (Psalm 36:8, emphasis added)

> "All my longings lie open before you, O Lord; my sighing is not hidden from you." (Psalm 38:9)

". . . My soul pants for you, O God. My soul thirsts for God, for the living God." (Psalm 42:1-2)

"I long to dwell in your tent forever and take refuge in the shelter of your wings." (Psalm 61:4, emphasis added)

"O God, you are my God, earnestly I seek you; my soul thirsts for you, my body longs for you, *in a dry and weary land where there is no water."* (Psalm 63:1, emphasis added)

"How lovely is your dwelling place, O Lord Almighty! My soul yearns, even faints, for the courts of the Lord; my heart and my flesh cry out for the living God" (Psalm 84:1-2, emphasis added).

Have mercy on me, O Lord, for I call to you all day long. *Bring joy to your servant, for to you, O Lord, I lift up my soul."* (Psalm 86:3-4, emphasis added)

"Hear my prayer, O Lord; let my cry for help come to you. *Do not hide your face from me when I am in distress. Turn your ear to me; when I call, answer me quickly."* (Psalm 102:1-2, emphasis added)

"He satisfies the thirsty and fills the hungry *with good things."* (Psalm 107:9, emphasis added)

"I spread my hands to you; my soul thirsts for you *like a parched land."* (Psalm 143:6, emphasis added)

My heart resonates with the intensity and the eagerness of the hymn writers' expressions of desire for God alone. The line which most accurately describes my own experience this year is Psalm 107:9: *"He satisfies the thirsty and fills the hungry with good things."* In the margin alongside this verse I wrote: "I have been praying ever since January 2000 that God will fill my heart with a hunger that only He can satisfy and stir my soul with a thirst which only He can quench." It's as though the Spirit of God branded my soul with a prayer that has persisted and continues to grow in intensity. What I have received from the Lord over these months are the *good things* He reserves for the hungry and the *rivers of delight* He gives to those who thirst (see Psalm 36:8).

> The bounty on His table will not diminish.

I need never fear that my hunger and thirst for God will outstrip His provision of spiritual food and drink. Should I live a thousand lifetimes and eat to the full daily, the bounty on His table will not diminish. As my desire for spiritual nourishment increases, my Father graciously introduces me to spiritual foods with flavors I had never tasted before. Let's not forget, however, that the *good things* and the *rivers of delight* are reserved for those who hunger and thirst for them. My only legitimate fear is that my hunger and thirst diminish, that I become careless and feed on things that can never satisfy my hunger or drink at fountains which cannot quench the deep longings of my soul. This is not to say that hunger and thirst for heavenly food is left entirely to me to generate. No. The Holy Spirit graciously creates hunger pangs and stirs the soul to eat and drink more and more of God's eternal words.

Meditating daily in the Bible's hymnbook inspired me to record personal heart-hungers in the form of written prayers. Here are three such prayers from the margins of my Cambridge NIV Bible:

An Intense Longing for the Presence of God

Holy Father, I resonate with David's plea. I, too, desire to remain in Your presence all the days of my life. Often I would much rather remain in my study to commune with You, to hear Your voice and to see Your face than to go to the office or to the airport on another trip.

Lord, I long for David's single, focused desire to sense Your presence. He asked for but one thing, not a grocery list of miscellaneous, self-

centered requests. 0, my Lord, when I sense Your presence, You have given me the ultimate. I am determined never to interrupt my pursuit of a conscious sense of Your presence. Open my eyes to see Your glory, Your unsurpassed beauty. I am not content simply to learn more about You or to receive Your good and perfect gifts. It is You I yearn to know; it is You I long to see. Come, my loving Lord, take me into Your strong, gentle arms and hold me securely; draw me tightly against Your breast. My wonderful Lord, I have been asking for even a glimpse of Your glory, of Your matchless beauty. Your Holy Spirit is the one who prompted this prayer. O that You would answer this prayer soon. Today, Lord? O that it would be today! Amen.

A Deep Desire to See the Lord

My gracious, loving Lord, when I read that the upright will see Your face, my heart is filled with joy, hope, and eager anticipation. Surely I shall soon see the beauty, splendor, and majesty of Your face. To gaze on Your face for even a moment will be worth a lifelong wait. My beautiful Lord Jesus Christ, You choose the time and the place for this ultimate encounter with You; prepare me for this moment of moments when my eyes shall actually see You. Touch my eyes to take in the brilliance of Your beauty, and purify my heart to take in Your holiness. I am totally unworthy and unfit to gaze upon Your lovely face, but I must see You, my Lord. O Lord, one glimpse of Your beauty will satisfy the longings of an entire lifetime. I do not ask to see You to bolster my faith, for I am more in love with You now than ever before, and more a convert to Your eternal truths than at any time in my life. I need not see You to believe, but I must see You because I love You. My longing becomes more intense; my hunger for You grows stronger. O my Lord, I love You, adore You, worship You, and exalt You. Search my heart and purify my motives behind this longing to see You. If need be, let my glimpse of Your glory end my life, but do not hide Your face from me. Amen.

A Prayer for the Nearness of God

Loving Lord, You are the one I seek. I long for a sense of Your presence in every conversation, in every communication, in every decision. My most diligent pursuit is to find You, to hear You, to see You. I am truly grateful for Your generous provision. Every good thing in my life comes from Your vast storehouse. But, dear Lord, more and more it is You that I seek; I long for You more than for all of Your good gifts. An intimate relationship with You is of infinitely greater worth to me than the bounty of Your gifts. My Lord, I long to worship up close and not at a distance. Take everything else from me, but give me the most intimate relationship with You. Cleanse me, purify me, discipline me, sanctify me. Prepare me to come very near—as close as the apostle John on Your breast; as near as Mary sitting at Your feet totally focused on Your words; as intimate as Abraham, Your friend with whom You shared Your plans; as close as Moses at the burning bush; as near as Enoch walking intimately with You when You took him. With my whole heart I seek such nearness to You, my Lord. Amen.

Heart-hunger leads to the deepest satisfaction.

My dear brothers and sisters, be reminded that we cannot hope to cultivate a heart-hunger for God through an occasional, casual moment of communion with Him. If your heart is not hungry for God, be concerned, very concerned, for it is when our devotion to Jesus Christ is at the lowest ebb that we are the most vulnerable to sin. Heart-hunger is the joyous state of being that results from a diligent, relentless pursuit, and from importunate pleas to our heavenly Father to satisfy our hunger and quench our thirst. Heart-hunger leads to the deepest satisfaction, for the more we eat, the more He spreads before us. Heart-hunger is itself one of the gifts He longs to give to you. When you seek after God with diligence, you will surely find Him. He is totally attentive to those who plead with Him for a hungry heart.

INTIMACY WITH GOD THROUGH THE PURSUIT OF HIS PLEASURE

Jesus modeled intimacy with His Father by seeking His pleasure. Never once did Jesus think, speak, or act so as to displease His Father (John 5:30). On the contrary, by His own testimony, He always did the things that pleased His Father (see John 8:29). Jesus' desire to gladden the heart of God was reciprocated, for the Father was also completely pleased with His Son. At His baptism the Father announced publicly, *"This is my Son, whom I love; with him I am well pleased"* (Matthew 3:17; Mark 1:11; Luke 3:22). The Father made a similar statement after Jesus' transfiguration (Matthew 17:5) but added the words, *"Listen to Him."* In essence God was saying, "My Son, Jesus, has my unreserved endorsement. I love Him. Our Father-Son relationship gives me great pleasure. Pay attention to His teaching. Obey Him!"

Think of it! Jesus' total life was focused on pleasing the Father who had sent Him on a mission among us. Jesus never lost sight of this mission for even one moment. The Father's agenda was Jesus' agenda. He lived His days by His Father's timetable. He did not speak or act on His own. Even as a child Jesus had a sense of the Father's mission (see Luke 2:49). When Jesus faced the supreme test, He chose the cross and the Father's will over His own (see Matthew 26:42; Mark 14:36; Luke 22:42). He pleased the Father by His obedience to Him.

I have pondered Jesus' life lived totally for the Father's pleasure. Should I follow in the steps of Jesus to live my life completely for God's pleasure? Should seeking my gracious heavenly Father's pleasure every day in everything also be my pursuit? My passion? My purpose for existence? If I am pursuing an intimate relationship with God, the answer is an unqualified yes! The deeper I go in my love for God, the more intense my desire is to please Him. The more diligent my pursuit of intimacy with the Almighty, the more powerful is the longing to please Him. Ultimately, His approval, His pleasure, and His joy matter more than anything else. The approval of man is worthless compared with my Father's favor. Like Jesus, I too am God's child, His son. Like Jesus, I too long to please my heavenly Father.

> The approval of man is worthless compared with my Father's favor.

On March 7, 1999 I wrote this prayer in the margin of my Bible alongside God's declaration of pleasure with His Son at His baptism: "My gracious, loving heavenly Father. It is my fervent prayer that You will be pleased with me. What can I do to please You? What will gladden Your heart and bring You pleasure? Is it not prompt and joyous obedience? Is it not complete trust in You? Help me to obey without hesitation and to trust without condition so that I can please You. May it be so." To this day, God's pleasure continues to be my prayerful pursuit.

Two Bible characters that sought to please God were Enoch and Moses. I've written an entire essay about Enoch's devotion ("Intimacy with God and Walking with God" on pg. 217), and the example of Moses has much to teach us as well. For Moses the presence of God was the surest indication that God was pleased with him.

His question of God was, *"How will anyone know that you are pleased with me and with your people unless you go with us"* (Exodus 33:16). The distinguishing mark of God's pleasure with Moses, even

> The distinguishing mark of God's pleasure with Moses would be His manifest presence.

among the surrounding nations, would be His manifest presence. Moses was determined not to take even one step in the direction of the Promised Land unless two things were settled—God's pleasure and His presence. God's assuring response was that His presence would indeed go with Moses because God said, *"I am pleased with you"* (Exodus 33:17). Accompanying God's pleasure would be His presence.

There are other examples of seeking God's pleasure in the Bible. Writing to the Corinthians, Paul said, *"We make it our goal to please him"* (2 Corinthians 5:9) and in his letter to the Ephesian Christians he urged them to *"find out what pleases the Lord"* (Ephesians 5:10).

The title of this piece is simply "Intimacy with God through the Pursuit of His Pleasure." This thought may seem a bit foreign to us. Since God is God and we are His creatures, we think more of the pleasure we derive from Him. We tend not to think in terms of His pleasure. Even with these few thoughts, I am confident that we will all agree that seeking God's pleasure is an important theme in the Scriptures. It is simply another way of defining a diligent pursuit of intimacy with God, i.e., going progressively deeper in knowing, loving, and serving God by intentionally committing to please Him.

INTIMACY WITH GOD AND KNOWING JESUS CHRIST

The apostle Paul said, *"I want to know Christ, and the power of his resurrection and the fellowship of sharing in his sufferings, becoming like him in his death"* (Philippians 3:10).

Saul of Tarsus became the unrivaled rising star in Judaism. In his preconversion days, he was viewed as a well-connected religious zealot. His résumé bulged with enviable credentials. For example, he came from a pure Jewish bloodline with a prestigious Benjamite ancestry; he had a strict religious upbringing from birth, and served as a "card-carrying" member of the fundamentalist sect of Pharisees. As an observer of Moses' Law, he was a meticulous practitioner of its minutest detail. Gamaliel, the maestro theologian in Israel, tutored Saul. He proved his zeal as a tireless inquisitor of the Christian church. With such a résumé, Saul seemed destined to go far.

Then his whole life turned upside down. His allegiance shifted. His life assignment changed radically. The only explanation for turning his back on so much potential promise would be the discovery of something or someone infinitely more compelling. That was indeed the case! Saul became a devoted follower of Jesus of Nazareth, the Messiah. He exchanged his boundless zeal for Judaism for a lifelong passion to know Jesus Christ, his Lord.

As Paul reflected on his past, everything he had valued and passionately pursued lost its luster. Writing about this he said, *"I consider everything a loss compared to the* surpassing greatness of knowing Christ Jesus my Lord" *(Philippians 3:8).* He went so far as to describe his preconversion achievements as vile refuse, as garbage, or even as dung. What an about-face! What a radical conversion! What a transformation! In his conversion encounter on the road to Damascus, Paul's passion shifted from a cause to a Person, from defending a legalistic religion to preaching the life-transforming gospel, from blaspheming Jesus Christ as an imposter to proclaiming Him as the eternal Son of God, and from seeking to destroy the churches to multiplying them.

At what point in Paul's life did he declare his passion to know Jesus Christ? He did so in a Roman prison nearing the time of his execution. For thirty years since his dramatic encounter with Jesus, knowing, loving, and serving Jesus Christ had been his perpetual pursuit. He never wavered in his quest for intimacy with Jesus Christ. This same passion to know Jesus Christ personally sustained Paul throughout his entire missionary career. What point am I making? Paul realized that the wonderful love relationship he had with Jesus Christ must continue to grow until the moment he stepped into His presence.

> The passion of Jesus' followers must remain Jesus.

The passion of Jesus' followers must remain Jesus. There can be no substitute, even for a short while. Whenever we love our work for Jesus more than Jesus Himself, we misplace our affections. In this intimate relationship with Jesus Christ, there are deeper depths and higher heights to achieve. Conversion is glorious, but it is only the beginning. A child in kindergarten may feel quite satisfied with early, elementary discoveries not realizing that learning the letters and numbers is but the smallest of beginnings. We cannot claim to be swimming with but one toe in the water. Neither can we claim spiritual maturity with just a basic knowledge of the Christian ABCs. What a tragic loss for a child of God to go through life quite oblivious to the sheer delight of a growing love relationship with Jesus Christ. What a tragedy to remain stuck in the introductory "conversion chapter" of life and never move on with intentional, disciplined, progressive steps toward intimacy with God.

In these essays on intimacy with God, we have said repeatedly that the primary way to grow in Christ is to go progressively deeper in knowing Him. By knowing Him we mean recognizing His distinct voice among a thousand clamoring voices, communing with Him in unhurried conversation, gazing on the brilliance of His beauty, discerning and embracing His perfect will, delighting in His holy presence, trusting Him without question, and obeying

> To know Christ is to love Him; to love Christ is to serve Him.

promptly whatever He asks of us. To know Christ is to love Him; to love Christ is to serve Him. To know Him is to enjoy a deepening love relationship with Him. It is all about pleasure or enjoyment. We gravitate toward the most enjoyable pleasure. When the child of God finds pure pleasure in his love relationship with Jesus Christ, all temporary, fake pleasures will lose their allure.

The apostle Paul paid dearly when he shifted his allegiance to Jesus Christ. Knowing Jesus intimately cost him everything, eventually his very life. His former fellow Pharisees now set out to kill him. While spreading the gospel on his three recorded missionary journeys, he amassed a résumé of sufferings unsurpassed by Christian missionaries of all time. Throughout his missionary career, he remained resolute in His passion to know Jesus Christ intimately. Paul viewed either life or death as advantages. In this life, knowing Jesus Christ was his passion.

Should he be killed or die a natural death, he would gain an even more intimate relationship with His Savior in His very presence.

Related to Paul's desire to know Jesus Christ intimately was an intense parallel desire to know the *"power of his resurrection and the fellowship of sharing in his sufferings, becoming like him in his death"* (Philippians 3:10). What did Paul mean? We cannot hope to understand what Paul meant by wanting to know Christ until we probe deeply into the sufferings, death, and resurrection of Jesus Christ.

The Power of His Resurrection

God demonstrated His ultimate power through the resurrection of Jesus Christ. Through His resurrection, Jesus conquered sin, death, and hell. To know Jesus Christ is to draw on that same resurrection power to live a victorious Christian life. By tapping into the power unleashed by Jesus' resurrection, we can be overcomers. If death, the ultimate power in Satan's arsenal, could not conquer Jesus, neither can Satan defeat us. Jesus' victory over death is also our victory.

The Fellowship of His Sufferings

Paul realized that to know Christ and to identify with Him also meant to *share* in His sufferings. The servant of Christ must expect the same treatment given to his Master. The more two people share in common, the more intimately they will know each other. For Paul, knowing Jesus Christ intimately would mean entering into His sufferings. His Lord was the Man of Sorrows. Without this intimate fellowship with the suffering Savior, the apostle Paul could not have endured so much suffering.

Like Him in His Death

To know Christ intimately may mean making the supreme sacrifice and actually dying for Him. Paul's intimate knowledge of Christ filled his being with total peace about the likelihood (the expectation?) of martyrdom. There is something more, however. Notice Paul's exact words: "becoming *like him* in his death" (Philippians 3:10, emphasis added). As he faced death, Jesus prayed the same prayer three times, *"Not my will but Yours be done."* In His death, Jesus was totally obedient to the Father. The Father's agenda was His agenda. Paul wanted to be like Jesus in his death, i.e., lifelong, prompt obedience to the perfect will of God.

Think for a moment of the *loftiest* possible pursuit to which you could devote a lifetime. Would it be to become a truly generous philanthropist, a world famous heart surgeon, a renowned professor of physics, a much loved head of state? Whatever it is, to have a reputation among those who know us best as one who knows Jesus Christ intimately is infinitely *loftier*.

Alternatively, reflect intently on the *ultimate life goal*, the goal that is sure to fill you with satisfaction when you look back on its achievement. Would it be to discover a cure for AIDS? To become the most published author in your generation? To be a husband and father whose wife honors him and whose children want to be like him? To revel in the privilege of being the first missionary to take the gospel to an unreached people group? Whatever you come up with, to know Jesus Christ intimately is far out front as the *ultimate life goal*. Whatever else you do, give yourself completely to achieving the ultimate life goal of knowing Jesus Christ. There simply is not a grander goal than to devote one's entire life to building a love relationship with Jesus Christ.

> To know Jesus Christ intimately is far out front as the ultimate life goal.

As a devoted follower of Jesus Christ, do I want to invest my life to gain the loftiest pursuit or to fulfill the ultimate life goal? Then I must be willing to invest time, energy, determination, discipline, and focus into knowing Jesus Christ intimately. Knowing Jesus the way Paul did is a lifelong quest; it is an all-consuming daily pursuit. It must be given permanent first place.

INTIMACY WITH GOD AND ACTS OF DEVOTION

I remember Mary of Bethany as a woman of deep devotion to Jesus Christ. In three separately-recorded incidents, we find her at Jesus' feet. Each scene adds a unique dimension to her devotion to Jesus Christ. There is no question but that Mary loved Jesus with all of her heart. She was a wholly-devoted, uninhibited, unashamed disciple of Jesus.

Mary lived with her older sister Martha and her brother Lazarus in Bethany, a village less than two miles from Jerusalem. Jesus frequented Bethany, especially during the final days leading up to His crucifixion. Apart from the meal in the home of Simon the Leper, Jesus' Bethany activities took place in the home of Martha and Mary. The two sisters were prominent women, for Bethany was known as the *"village of Mary and Martha"* (John 11:1). Apparently they were also well known in Jerusalem, the big city nearby, for when Lazarus died, their many Jewish friends walked from Jerusalem to Bethany to comfort the two sisters (see John 11:19).

After Jesus raised Lazarus from the dead, even larger crowds of people filled the narrow streets around Mary and Martha's village home. All Jerusalem came to catch a glimpse of Lazarus of Bethany who had been dead for four days and was now alive and well. It matters not that Bethany was a small village. Just like crowds of people flocked to hear

John the Baptist in the wilderness, so they came to humble Bethany to see Lazarus who exhibited the most amazing demonstration of Jesus' power.

Spending Time in Jesus' Presence

Jesus' first visit to the home of Mary and Martha in Bethany may well be the one where Martha served while Mary sat at Jesus' feet to listen to His teaching. In her view, housework could wait, not because it wasn't important, but compared with spending time listening to Jesus, it was less of a priority. Domestic chores could wait, but learning from Jesus could not. Tomorrow, the next day, and even the next would still be adequate time to do housework, but opportunities to be instructed by Jesus did not come every day.

When her older sister complained that Mary wasn't shouldering her share of the work around the house, Jesus came to Mary's defense. He was not making a statement about the importance of housework. He was, however, gently reminding Martha that her younger sister's decision to listen to His teaching was the best choice, the benefits of which no one could ever take away. *Mary's first recorded act of devotion to Jesus was a deliberate decision to listen intently to Him.* Her soul thirsted for more and more of Jesus' teaching. Her heart hungered for the living words of Jesus. She hungered for spiritual food. She became totally engrossed in what Jesus had to say. Little wonder she had insights that even some of Jesus' immediate disciples did not have. The teachings of Jesus are like the fountainhead for a life completely devoted to Jesus Christ.

> The teachings of Jesus are like the fountainhead for a life completely devoted to Jesus Christ.

Lest we judge Martha too harshly, let me set the record straight for the "Marthas" in our world. Their service is both important and appreciated. We could not function without the help of a Martha-mind-set. Not all who serve are given to anxiety over their service like Martha of Bethany was. Some "Marthas" demonstrate their devotion to Jesus by the sacrificial work of their hands. They are able to bake bread, clean the house, or do the laundry as an act of devotion to Jesus Christ. We might say that they have a balanced blend of Martha's hands and Mary's heart.

Bringing Our Sorrow and Grief to Jesus

Prior to a second visit to Bethany, Mary and Martha sent a message to Jesus to inform Him that their brother Lazarus, the one whom Jesus loved, was very ill. They knew to whom to turn in this time of crisis. Jesus responded to their cry for help, but not till Lazarus was dead and his body placed in a stone-covered burial cave for four full days. Both sisters' words, *"Lord, if you had been here, my brother would not have died"* (John 11:21, 32) suggested that in their view the time for Jesus to act had passed. They thought they knew how Jesus must perform a miracle on their behalf. Now it seemed too late for Jesus' power to be demonstrated. What they had in mind was a restoration to health; what Jesus had in mind was a resurrection to life itself.

When Jesus came, Martha went outside the village to receive Him and His disciples. Seeing Jesus, she had a conversation with Him about Lazarus' future resurrection. Martha's theology was straight as an arrow. Like Peter, Martha confessed that Jesus was the Christ the Son of God.

As for Mary, we find her once again at Jesus' feet, her characteristic posture in Jesus' presence. The apostle John tells us that when she saw Jesus, she fell at his feet, this time not to listen to His teaching, but to pour out the anguish of her soul. This too was an act of devotion to Jesus. *Mary's second act of devotion was bringing the heaviness of heart to Jesus and in this way demonstrating her total trust in Him.* With whom else could she share her grief? Her tears and convulsive sobbing erupted like a pent-up torrent of emotion. "Jesus, if you had only been here, this would not have happened." Mary's tears moved Jesus deeply. Moments later the two sisters' brother, Lazarus, was miraculously raised from the dead.

Devoting Our Best to Jesus

The third and final scene of Mary at the feet of Jesus took place less than a week before Jesus' substitutionary death on the cross. Ever since the raising of Lazarus from the dead, the little village of Bethany had gained the reputation of the place "where Lazarus lived." The two sisters now gave a dinner in Jesus' honor. They wanted to express their deep gratitude to Jesus for raising their brother from the dead. Predictably, Martha served. Serving was her passion. Lazarus was among the guests of honor and reclined at the table near to Jesus. The apostle John does not tell us about other guests, but since it was an event in honor of Jesus, I visualize an open house for all who lived in Bethany; in addition to honoring Jesus, the two sisters were evangelizing their neighbors.

In the middle of the meal, Mary interrupted what otherwise might have been remembered as a fairly routine event. Prompted by a deep love for Jesus, Mary took a pint of fragrant ointment and anointed Jesus' feet. Both the meal and the conversation ceased. We have no recorded words spoken by Mary in this incident. No matter. Devotion to Jesus Christ is spoken in the heart language of loving, sacrificial deeds and not in the

> True acts of devotion aren't announced or advertised.

eloquent platitudes of the lips. Mary strikes me to be a listener more than a speaker. Isn't there a correlation between the art of listening and acts of devotion? True acts of devotion aren't announced or advertised. Not even one person knows what Mary may have said, but literally millions of Christians from many lands for over two thousand years have been moved by this account of Mary's love for Jesus. Our impression of

Mary is that she preferred the shadows to the limelight. It was totally uncharacteristic for her to even try to "steal the show" at a public banquet, but what she did for Jesus gave her a permanent lead part in the company of Jesus' faithful followers.

This is such a breathtaking scene that we must look at it again. What really happened? From the apostle John's account, we picture Mary breaking into the middle of the banquet conversation, kneeling at Jesus' feet, deliberately taking a flask of pure perfume and pouring it over His feet. Then, as the pleasing fragrance wafted through the entire house, she proceeded to wipe His feet with her hair. For at least a moment, Mary's act of devotion brought all conversation to a halt. Suddenly, every eye was riveted on Mary on her knees wiping Jesus' feet with her hair. To attend to the feet of a guest was the task of the lowliest household slave. *Mary's final act of devotion to Jesus Christ was her sacrificial giving of her best to Jesus.*

As I read this account of Mary's humble devotion, I am surprised that Jesus' disciples and at least some of the dinner guests did not also fall to their knees before Jesus. At the very least, one would have expected some affirmation for Mary from those who witnessed this unusual act of devotion to Jesus. But there was nothing of the kind. Instead, it was Judas' immediate outrage and objection to what he viewed as reckless extravagance that broke the silence.

Feigning concern for the poor, Judas asked why the perfume wasn't sold and the proceeds given to those who lacked food, clothing, and shelter. Judas was claiming that he had a better use for the ointment worth a whole year's wages. Jesus saw past his pious words to a stingy, calculating heart. Judas' love for money became the beachhead for Satan's fateful invasion into his soul.

Jesus now came to Mary's defense for the second time. His words, *leave her alone,* are a stinging rebuke, first to Judas, and then today to all who think that sacrificial devotion to Jesus is a waste. They do not understand the strong compulsion of a heart full of love and gratitude. Love is not love, and devotion is not devotion, if it calculates the cost. In our day they would be among the first to cry "what a waste" when a young couple abandons a promising career with big salary and benefits to become missionaries to an unreached people group.

Did Mary know that her sacrificial act of devotion was part of God's plan and that Jesus viewed what she did as preparation for His burial? It's not likely that she did. Often our acts of devotion to Jesus have far-reaching ramifications we neither planned nor expected. The fragrance of Mary's act of devotion filled more than the house in Bethany. It has spread throughout the entire world. Neither did Mary know that this was her last opportunity to anoint Jesus before His

> It's important that we follow the impulses of our heart to engage in acts of devotion.

death. In our case too, it's important that we follow the impulses of our heart to engage in acts of devotion while there is still opportunity.

There are some important twenty-first century lessons to be learned from Mary's beautiful example of generous devotion to Jesus Christ. Such devotion springs spontaneously from a heart . . .

- that has been drinking long and intently at the fountain of Jesus' teaching
- that has made an intentional choice to put time with Jesus ahead of everything else
- that is undivided and undistracted in its devotion to Jesus Christ
- that is overwhelmed with gratitude for all Jesus has done for her/ him
- that is not attached to material things but gives them up freely to demonstrate love for Jesus Christ
- that is motivated by love and gratitude for Jesus and not by recognition from man

- that cares little about the cost behind a sacrificial act of devotion to Jesus Christ so long as the best is given to Him.

We do not have Jesus' physical presence with us today. We cannot engage in precisely the same kind of acts of devotion Mary did. We do, however, have Jesus' pledge that He views loving acts of kindness done for others in His Name as though done directly for Him. Giving drink to the thirsty, food to the hungry, clothing to the naked, and hospitality to the stranger, or visiting the sick and prison inmates can all be sacrificial acts of devotion to Jesus Christ (see Matthew 25:34-40).

In Mary we have an example of one who was diligent in her pursuit of intimacy with God. How did she develop such a relationship? She did so by spending time in Jesus' presence listening to Him, by bringing the heavy matters in life to Jesus, and by holding back nothing of value from Jesus. She listened to Jesus, cast her cares upon Jesus, and gave her best to Jesus.

INTIMACY WITH GOD AND DOING WHAT IS RIGHT AND JUST

What does the LORD require of you? To act justly and to love mercy and to walk humbly with your God. (Micah 6:8)

In this series of essays, I have defined intimacy with God as going progressively deeper in knowing, loving, and serving God. The order in these three steps is both sequential and intentional. We cannot love the God we do not know and we will not long serve the God we do not love.

Knowing almighty God is the first step toward an intimate relationship with Him. Since knowing God leads to loving Him and

> One way to know God is to engage in conduct that is both right and just.

loving God leads to serving Him, it is imperative that we focus much effort and energy on knowing God intimately. One way to know God is to engage in conduct that is both right and just.

Good King Josiah illustrates the connection between knowing God and doing what is right; that is, living a righteous life. He is described as doing what was *"right in the eyes of the LORD"* (2 Kings 22:2). In his sweeping reforms to undo the evil done by his grandfather Manasseh during his fifty-five year reign, it was said of Josiah: *"Neither before or after Josiah was there a king like him who turned to the LORD as he did—with all his* heart *and with all his* soul *and with all his* strength, *in accordance with all the Law of Moses"* (2 Kings 23:25). What a reputation! What a living legacy to leave for posterity! Among all of the kings of Judah, including David and Hezekiah, both before and after him, Josiah stood tallest in his devotion to God and in his zeal for God's cause. In his devotion to God, Josiah was a giant and worthy of our emulation many centuries later.

In addition to doing what was right, Josiah also did what was just. Through the prophet Jeremiah, God said that Josiah did what was right and just, and as a result all went well with him. God was pleased with Josiah's righteousness and just conduct. We already know what Josiah did to be called a righteous king, but what did he do that warrants God's calling him just? In God's own words, it was to *"[defend] the poor and needy"* (Jeremiah 22:16). His devotion and zeal for God became the wellspring of his advocacy for the poor and needy.

In sharp contrast Jehoiakim, Josiah's successor son, lived an opulent life by exploiting the poor. He had his palace with spacious upper rooms and large bay windows built by *"making his countrymen work for nothing."* His eyes and his heart were totally materialistic and consumed with greed. He had no scruples about shedding innocent blood and extorting from the poor the little they had. God could not tolerate such a heartless, merciless leader, so He had him removed from the throne. Jehoiakim's reign lasted only three months before he was taken captive to Egypt where he eventually died.

Surely there is a connection between doing what was right and acting justly. Those who live a righteous life like Josiah did will be more likely to defend the poor and the needy. Out of the overflow of their deep communion with God, those who have established an intimate walk with God will more likely engage in acts of justice. Josiah's son Jehoiakim lived an evil life. It should not surprise us that he also exploited the poor.

God followed His assessment of Josiah's conduct with an astounding rhetorical question: *"Is this not what it means to know me?"* (Jeremiah

22:16). "This" refers back to defending the poor and needy, so the answer to God's question is a resounding yes! There is indeed a direct link between treating the poor justly and knowing God intimately. An important way to know God intimately is to openly use our resources and influence to defend the poor and the needy and to

> There is indeed a direct link between treating the poor justly and knowing God intimately.

become an advocate for the helpless, disenfranchised people of our world. Do you want to know God more intimately? Defending the poor and needy is one practical way to establish an intimate walk with God.

Both in His character and through His acts, almighty God Himself is a champion of the poor, the needy, the widow, the orphan, and the helpless. Consider these clear statements in the Psalms about our heavenly Father's heart for those with special needs:

- "The LORD *is a refuge for the oppressed"* (Psalm 9:9, emphasis added).
- God defends *"the fatherless and the oppressed"* (Psalm 10:18, emphasis added).
- "You [God] rescue the poor from those too strong for them, the poor and needy from those who rob from them" (Psalm 35:10).
- God is *"a father* to the fatherless, a defender of widows" (Psalm 68:5, emphasis added).
- "From your bounty, O God, you provided for the poor" (Psalm 68:10).
- "Defend the cause of the weak and fatherless; maintain the rights of the poor and the oppressed. Rescue the weak and the needy; deliver them from the hand of the wicked" (Psalm 82:3-4).
- "He raises the poor from the dust and lifts the needy from the ash heap; he seats them . . . with the princes of their people" (Psalm 113:7-8).
- "I know that the LORD secures justice for the poor and upholds the cause of the needy" (Psalm 140:12).

• *"He upholds the cause of the oppressed and gives food to the hungry. The* L*ORD sets prisoners free, the* L*ORD gives sight to the blind, the* L*ORD lifts up those who are bowed down, the* L*ORD loves the righteous. The* L*ORD watches over the alien and sustains the fatherless and the widow"* (Psalm 146:7-9).

What a powerful sequence of Scriptural statements! What do they teach us? They make crystal clear that the objects of our faithful Father's provision, deliverance, healing, justice, restoration, defense, and advocacy are the widows, orphans, aliens, prisoners, oppressed, poor, needy, and weak. This is the list of people close to God's heart. Our God and Father has already taken full note of each person in need. We cannot claim a place close to God's heart without also being close to the likes of the people on God's list.

As evangelicals we may be in danger of pursuing a life of devotion to God and at the same time neglecting issues of justice for the poor. James, the brother of our Lord, reminds us that the *"religion that our Father accepts as pure and faultless is this: to look after orphans and widows in their distress and to keep oneself from being polluted by the world"* (James 1:27). On the one hand we must see to the needs of the homeless (orphaned children and refugees) and the helpless, and on the other hand we are compelled to live a holy life of separation from the corruptions of this world. In other words, like Josiah, we must live righteously and act justly.

Dorcas had two outstanding qualities: she was a disciple of Jesus Christ *"who was always doing good and helping the poor"* (Acts 9:36). The two go together—devotion to Jesus Christ as His follower and doing good by helping the poor.

Where does the motivation to minister to the poor come from? It will never come from our self-centered hearts. The most we can muster in our own strength is sympathy, and in our occasional better moments, even empathy. To love the poor genuinely and to help them effectively, we must be compelled or motivated by God's love. In other words, the fountainhead or wellspring of a heart of compassion for the poor and needy is an intimate walk with God.

> The fountainhead or wellspring of a heart of compassion for the poor and needy is an intimate walk with God.

Let's get practical. We need not travel far to find the poor and needy. Our inner cities abound with the poor. Our next door neighbors might well be on God's list as poor people. With every armed international conflict the result is an escalating number of refugees. What are refugees? They are helpless, harassed, hassled families—fractured families. On a global scale, the growing number of refugees housed in camps exceeds tens of millions. An estimated three-fourths of the world's HIV positive cases are in Africa. The vast majority of the AIDS-related deaths occur in Sub-Saharan Africa. Millions of children are orphaned each year because parents have either died or are no longer able to take care of their own. God sees their plight; they are the objects of the Father's mercy, compassion, and grace. They are given priority on our merciful Father's list. We cannot claim to have an intimate relationship with our compassionate Father and at the same time neglect the AIDS victims in Africa.

Do I want to know God more intimately? Then I must embrace His agenda for the poor and needy, and in so doing act righteously and justly. Do I want to come nearer to God? Then I must come closer to those who are on God's heart. Do I want to lay my head on His bosom like the apostle John did on Jesus' breast? If I do, I will discover that the poor are already there.

Loving Lord, grant me Your eyes to see the poor, Your heart to love them, and Your hands to minister to their needs.

INTIMACY WITH GOD AND WALKING IN THE LIGHT

But if we are living in the light of God's presence, just as Christ does, then we have wonderful fellowship and joy with each other, and the blood of Jesus his Son cleanses us from every sin. (1 John 1:7, TLB)

Jesus chose John to be *with Him* (see Mark 3:14). This *with Him* principle seems to have applied to John more than to the other apostles, for John lived his days nearer to Jesus than any of his fellow disciples. He was known as the disciple whom Jesus loved (see John 13:23; 19:26; 20:2; 21:7, 20, 24). It was John who reclined next to Jesus at their final meal together (see John 13:23), and when he talked with Jesus, He leaned against Him (see vs. 25). As a member of the inner circle of three apostles, John was near to Jesus constantly—on the Mount of Transfiguration (see Matthew 17:1-13), where he heard God the Father say of Jesus, *"This is my Son, whom I love; with him I am well pleased. Listen to Him!"* In the Garden of Gethsemane he witnessed Jesus' agony in prayer (see Matthew 26:36-46); he was near Jesus at His crucifixion (see John 19:26-27); he became one of the first eyewitnesses of the empty tomb and of the risen Christ (see John 20:3-9). John was so close to Jesus that he was chosen to take care of His mother, Mary.

There is no doubt about it. John knew Jesus intimately. He had heard Him, seen Him and touched Him (see 1 John 1:1). And now in his writings, he proclaims Jesus. John is well qualified to instruct us on intimacy with God. He speaks from personal experience. In his writings, John makes three theological statements about God's very essence. These three statements tell us what God is like and what an intimate relationship with Him will require of us.

God Is Light (John 1:5)

Therefore, to be in God's presence, we too must dwell in His light. Light denotes God's glory, brilliance, splendor, absolute purity, holiness, and truth. This light is so perfectly pure, there isn't even the tiniest speck of darkness in Him. Intimacy with God is impossible in the shadows, much less in the darkness. The pure light of God's presence exposes all sins of thought, word, and deed. A refusal to deal quickly with sin when exposed by the light of His presence is tantamount to a retreat back into the darkness.

God Is Spirit (John 4:24)

Therefore, I must approach Him not as an image with all of its impotence and limitations, but as the eternal, supreme God who is all powerful, all knowing, and everywhere present. God is a spiritual being: He is infinitely more than anything material. There can be no intimacy with God if I reduce Him to a likeness created by my own finite mind. You would not want the God devised by my limited mental powers, and I would be unwilling to settle for the God fashioned by anyone else's mind.

God Is Love (1 John 4:7-12)

Therefore, as God's child, I too must love *whom* God loves and *what* God loves. There can be no intimacy with God if I refuse to love my brothers and sisters or if my affections are centered on the fleeting things of this world (1 John 2:15-17). This is the God with whom we seek an intimate relationship.

But now, let us focus more specifically on our text. What does it mean to walk in the light as He is in the light? Briefly, walking in the light means . . .

- to live all my days in His pure presence
- to move steadily in the direction of purity and holiness
- to be progressively transformed into God's likeness
- to live in open and joyous relationships with my Christian brothers and sisters
- to allow the pure light of God's holiness to expose the darkness (sin) in me
- to fulfill my divine calling, for God has called me out of darkness into His wonderful light (see 1 Peter 2:9).

> Light must characterize our life in Christ.

Darkness describes our preconversion days (see Ephesians 5:8-9), but light must characterize our life in Christ, for we are now children of light. It is no longer necessary for us to grope and stumble in the darkness. We can walk confidently in the light.

We must not overlook the six words *as He is in the light* (see 1 John 1:7). This is nothing less than the very presence of God. All of our movements, all of our activities, all of our conversations, and all of our attitudes are to take place conscious of His presence. We must consciously and intentionally take everything we are, all we do, every thought, all fears, all motives, and all agendas into the light of His presence.

The two-fold outcome of *"walking in the light as He is in the light"* (1 John 1:7) is wonderful to contemplate. The first is fellowship with one another. John is speaking of Christian communion, brother-to-brother, sister-to-sister communion. Such fellowship is open, transparent, joyous, and without hidden agendas. Motives have been exposed to the light of God's presence.

It is important to understand that the true test of fellowship or intimacy with God is fellowship with my brothers and sisters. Just as love for God is reflected in my love for Christian brothers and sisters, so intimacy with God is demonstrated by the measure of true fellowship I have with those who are walking in the light with me. To say that I am going progressively deeper in knowing, loving, and serving God and at the same time to dwell in darkness in my relationship with my wife, husband, family member, co-worker, or neighbor, is to live a lie. Such a life has strayed from the light and into the shadows. It is impossible to have a relationship which is whole toward God and broken toward my brother. God's plan is for me to be in the light together with my brother and sister, never alone. If I have a relationship which is broken, I must take my brother or sister by the hand and together walk into the light of God's presence. There, in the brilliant light of His presence, all motives, resentments, and hidden fears will be exposed and dealt with. There, in the pure light of His presence, no sinful thought or motive will be worth retaining.

The second outcome of *walking in the light as He is in the light* is the ongoing cleansing from all sin through the blood of Jesus. Here is a wonderful truth. The finished work of Christ on the cross keeps on cleansing us from all sin. The present continuous tense of the verb means that I am being cleansed continuously. What power, what efficacy there is in the shed blood of Jesus! There is, of course, that initial application of Jesus' substitutionary death at salvation. But there is also the daily, moment-by-moment purifying power of the blood for the believer. John says to fellow believers: *"If anybody does sin, we have one who speaks*

> What power, what efficacy there is in the shed blood of Jesus!

to the Father in our defense—Jesus Christ, the Righteous One. He is the atoning sacrifice for our sins, and not only for ours but also for the sins of the whole world" (1 John 2:1-2). We do sin. We have not yet been fully sanctified, but the glorious truth is that we have Jesus, the Righteous One, as our Advocate before the Father. We also have His shed blood as the continuous covering for our sin.

As I conclude this piece on "Intimacy with God and Walking in the Light," my own heart longs for the light of God's presence. Further, there is a longing in my heart for such a walk for all of us who believe in and call upon the name of the Lord. Can you imagine the difference it would make if all who know Him personally also walked continuously in the light together, as He is in the light? We would be profoundly blessed and so would the world that desperately needs Jesus Christ, the Light of the World.

INTIMACY WITH GOD AND SOUL-SATISFYING FOOD

It's possible to be in excellent physical condition and at the same time starve the soul. We can eat vitamin-rich foods, walk, or jog regularly, maintain a slim figure, keep our HDL cholesterol level high and the LDL count low, and still stunt our spiritual growth. A malnourished child with distended belly is a tragic sight. How infinitely more serious not to keep our eternal soul supplied with spiritual sustenance, especially when it's available in such never-ending abundance.

God has planned that we be spiritually nourished in at least two ways—by feeding on His Word and by doing His work. God's Word and His work must not be viewed separately. We discover clear instructions for His work in the pages of His Word. The clearest road map for the work of God is the Word of God.

God's Word is the soul's staple food. Quoting Moses (see Deuteronomy 8:3), Jesus made it crystal clear that there are two types of food, one for the body and another for the soul: *"Man does not live on bread alone, but on every word that comes from the mouth of God"* (Matthew 4:4). Jesus is saying that there is a part of you those three meals a day will not feed; that it's possible to become a physical giant and remain a spiritual midget.

We know how bread nourishes the body, but how do we live on the

Word of God? Isn't it simply by obeying its precepts and living by its principles? Isn't it also by coming to the Bible regularly with the strong expectation that the Holy Spirit who inspired the Scriptures many centuries ago will speak through them again in the twenty-first century? Further, isn't it as I read meditatively that there will be instruction, exhortation, direction, and encouragement for me in my current situation? The Bible is not the soul's appetizer; it is its main course. To maintain a robust spiritual life, an occasional nibble or even a snack now and then will not suffice. No! Nothing should be allowed to keep us from enjoying repeated, regular, hearty meals of the soul-food Jesus urged us to eat.

> The Bible is not the soul's appetizer; it is its main course.

How does feeding on the Word of God contribute to intimacy with God? Is it not that through the Word He converses and communes with us? This is where we encounter God, where we go progressively deeper in knowing His character. This is also where we discover His way of dealing with us. George Müller insisted that it was much more important for God to speak to us than for us to speak to God. Given his reputation as a mighty man of prayer, this is compelling counsel. Near the end of his life, he reported to a friend that he had read the Bible through well over one hundred times. Recently I spoke with an esteemed friend who told me that he was reading through the Bible three times a year. What better way to know God more intimately than to pour over His eternal words in the Bible!

But it's not only the Word of God that nourishes the soul. For Jesus, doing the Father's work was also soul-food. He had just told the five-time married Samaritan woman about eternal, thirst-quenching water (John 4:7ff.). The unnamed woman left that conversation with Jesus convinced that He was the long-awaited Messiah. Apart from the apostle John, the disciples missed hearing this profound conversation with the woman at

Jacob's well, for they had gone to Sychar to purchase food. When they returned, they urged Jesus to eat. Surely He would be hungry, but He had no appetite for their food. He had *"food to eat"* that they did not understand (John 4:32). He went on to describe this "mystery food" as obedience to the will of God and as finishing His assignment (see John 4:34). To be renewed and energized by something other than physical food was new to the disciples and possibly to us as well.

Significantly, Jesus linked His mission to bringing in a spiritual harvest (see John 4:35-38). Lost people were at the heart of His mission (see Luke 19:10). Jesus' evangelistic labor in Samaria led to the conversion of the Samaritan woman and many Samaritan villagers. They now believed that Jesus was the *"Savior of the world"* (John 4:39, 42). Missionaries are "international harvesters" engaged in relentless, culturally appropriate evangelism. Bringing in the harvest or doing evangelism is the work that energized Jesus. Engaging in evangelism will do the same for us.

Let us join Jesus in "eating" the spiritual food of daily obedience within the sphere of our ministry assignments. Finishing the Father's work became the driving force in Jesus' life (see John 17:4). In the end He could say that He had finished all that the Father had given Him to do (see John 19:28). As long as we are occupied with our Father's work, it will be like food for us. Realizing that the work we do is fulfilling the purpose of God will sustain us in difficult times. It will also give us patience with the harvest which seems slow in coming. God's assignments are neither easy nor necessarily safe, but they satisfy the soul. You say that yours is an insignificant, out-of-the-way assignment and that it's of little consequence? How could that be since God Himself called you to do it? Could any task possibly be small if God is in it? On the other hand, the pursuit of our own agendas and the insistence of our own time frames will deplete our limited energies and ultimately wear us out.

At the outset of each new day, my prayer must be, *"Lord, today let me complete everything You have planned for me—no more, no less. Fill my soul with a sense of destiny about fulfilling Your purpose. Let every conversation, e-mail, decision, and new idea reflect Your plan for this day. In short, throughout this day, let Your agenda be my agenda. I am at Your disposal to do Your will. Let me be particularly alert to the unscheduled opportunities to be Your hands, feet, and mouth. Tonight, allow me to look back on a day marked by prompt, complete obedience and diligent service. Being able to do so will give me more delight than eating a sumptuous ten-course Chinese meal. Amen."*

What then is the link between intimacy with God and His mission? Is it not this, that as we engage in His work, we are working with Him? Difficult and overwhelming as it might be for us to grasp, we actually become partners, co-laborers with the God of the universe. The

> God alone can satisfy our spiritual hunger and quench our inner thirst.

realization that I am where I am because of divine appointment energizes me. His work fills me with a sense of divine destiny. I did not choose this task, nor did I choose to live here, but the Sovereign Lord of the vast universe personally selected good works for me to do (see Ephesians 2:10).

Ultimately, God alone can satisfy our spiritual hunger and quench our inner thirst. In fact, He is the One who creates cravings for both His Word and His work. We might say that He prepares the "meal" and then stimulates the appetite to enjoy it to the full. We do not naturally hunger for either the Word or work of God. If I have hunger for holiness or intimacy with God, if I have a passion to do His will, then I am singularly blessed. Such hunger represents the bestowal of one of His precious gifts. I say this because when it comes to the Scriptures, my mind is dull and drowsy. As for the work of God, I would be much more inclined to pursue my own ambitions. There is no hunger He stimulates which He does not also satisfy. It boils down to this. Our gracious heavenly Father does it all. He creates the craving and then spreads before us the most delicious of thirst-quenching and hunger-satisfying delights. But we must eat and drink, not hurriedly, but deliberately savoring each bite of the rich truths from God's holy Word and enjoying each moment of going about His work.

One of the most indicting illustrations of searching for soul satisfaction in the wrong place is recorded by Jeremiah about Israel. God leveled two complaints against His people: *"They have forsaken me, the spring of living water, and have dug their own cisterns, broken cisterns that cannot hold water"* (Jeremiah 2:13). They did the unthinkable by exchanging the almighty God for worthless idols (see Jeremiah 2:11). In the process they became like the objects of their worship (see Jeremiah 2:5. See also Psalm 115:8). They traded a sparkling water fountain for a leaky, underground storage tank, and a perennially fresh supply of spring water for putrid, algae-covered water. What a loser of a deal!

Before I point a finger at the Israelites, I must take inventory of my own life. Where do I go to satisfy my inner hunger and quench my deepest spiritual thirst? From which "wells" do I drink? What I do, read, watch, or hear can become either an artesian well or a polluted cistern. Do I substitute sitcoms, videos, novels, soaps, aimless surfing on the Internet, and sampling borderline materials for the fresh water spring of communion with God? If I do, the exchange is as bad as the Israelites trading God for the worthless idols. In the course of a week, do I spend more hours reading *Time, US News,* and *Newsweek* than poring over the Scriptures? True, I must be an informed leader, but when it comes to feeding my soul, the articles in these magazines are about as nourishing as eating Styrofoam. Do I devote more time listening to ABC's *World News* and Public Television's *News Hour* than to the Holy Spirit instructing my soul from God's Word? Again, I need the information, but the nightly news is no substitute for drinking deeply and frequently at God's "springs of living water."

Let's be done with digging cisterns. Let us turn our back on all unsatisfying substitutes. Why languish surrounded by a never-ending supply of spiritual food and drink? Can you imagine dying of thirst lying beside a spring-fed brook or starving to death in a supermarket? My dear brothers and sisters, dig in! *Bon appétit*! Let the Word and work of God nourish your soul!

INTIMACY WITH GOD AND SUFFERING

Two statements, one from Paul and one from Peter, link suffering to intimacy with God. Paul's passion was to *"know Christ and the power of His resurrection and the fellowship of sharing in his sufferings, becoming like him in his death"* (Philippians 3:10).

In our pursuit of intimacy with God, we eagerly join Paul in his desire to know Christ. Yes, of course, we want to go progressively deeper in knowing Him. We want to go beyond factual information about Jesus. We want to know Him! We also welcome the thought of experiencing His resurrection power in our ministries. But we shrink at the thought of *"sharing in His sufferings"* and *"becoming like Him in His death."*

> We shrink at the thought of *"sharing in His sufferings."*

Paul, on the other hand, was as passionate about sharing in Christ's sufferings as about knowing Him. In fact, Paul is saying that to know Christ and His resurrection power is impossible apart from also sharing in His sufferings—the suffering which comes from misunderstanding, unjust treatment, ridicule, and rejection. Jesus walked the Calvary road. Do we think that we can have an intimate relationship with Him and not walk with Him?

We tend to think it remarkable that the early followers of Jesus rejoiced because they were considered worthy to suffer disgrace for Christ (Acts 5:41). They expected suffering. Their Master had suffered, so why shouldn't they? Suffering opposition was more the norm than the unusual. Suffering was not and is not abnormal.

Peter also links suffering to intimacy with Christ: *"Dear friends,"* he wrote, *"do not be surprised at the painful trial you are suffering, as though something strange were happening to you. But rejoice that you* participate in the sufferings of Christ, *so that you may be overjoyed when his glory is revealed"* (1 Peter 4:12-13). We gladly experience Christ in His glory, but we have second thoughts about partnering with Him in His sufferings. The Puritans said of suffering, "No pain, no gain." Peter seems to be saying, "No suffering, no glory."

An important lesson about the linkage between suffering and intimacy with God is that suffering can actually be part of God's plan for us. That comes as a shock to affluent Americans who view comfort and ease as inalienable rights. I can undergo intense suffering and still be in the very epicenter of God's perfect will for me. Peter says as much: *"Those who suffer according to God's will should commit themselves to their faithful Creator and continue to do good!"* (1 Peter 4:19, emphasis added). Peter's counsel is not to ask for deliverance from suffering, but to place ourselves into God's hand and at the same time stay the course in doing good.

> Suffering can actually be part of God's plan for us.

If honest, we would all admit that we come much closer to God during times of trial and affliction. We pray more. We cry to God for deliverance. We search the Scriptures more diligently. Our grip on the passing things of this world is loosened. Our perspectives change. Surely these are benefits of unsurpassed value.

Hezekiah recognized his suffering in deathbed sickness as good for him: *"Surely it was for my benefit that I suffered such anguish"* (Isaiah 38:17). Solomon also recognized the great value of suffering: *"Blows and wounds cleanse away evil, and beatings purge the inmost being"* (Proverbs 20:30).

Perhaps the clearest series of statements on the eternal value of suffering is in Psalm 119.

1. Suffering restores us to the right path. *"Before I was afflicted I went astray, but now I obey your word"* (vs. 67).

2. Suffering leads to new insights into the meaning and application of God's Word. *"It was good for me to be afflicted so that I might learn your decrees"* (vs. 71).

3. Suffering demonstrates God's faithfulness. *"In faithfulness you have afflicted me"* (vs. 75).

4. Suffering brings out the keeping power of God's Word. *"If your law had not been my delight, I would have perished in my affliction"* (vs. 92).

In our pursuit of intimacy with God, we may not have known about its tie to suffering. The two are inseparably linked. They were for Jesus. He suffered in Gethsemane and on Calvary—both in the Father's will.

INTIMACY WITH GOD AND ANXIETY

The Lord is near. Do not be anxious about anything, but in everything, by prayer and petition, with thanksgiving, present your requests to God. And the peace of God, which transcends all understanding, will guard your hearts and minds in Christ Jesus. (Philippians 4:5-7)

Quite honestly, Paul's words have seemed beyond reach to me. Is it really possible to reach a state of zero anxiety or a mental condition where there is no uneasiness or sense of foreboding about anything?

Paul isn't simply saying it would be nice not to worry about an uncertain future. His imperative is clear: *"Do not be anxious about anything."* In other words, there is no situation whether present or future which should be allowed to give us mental pain.

Take any situation we face. On the side of anxiety there is to be a zero, but on the other side of the "ledger" every situation is to be presented to God through thankful prayer and petition. The stress comes when we reverse the order—100 percent on the side of anxiety and zero on the side of prayer to God. The divine formula is simply this: worry about nothing, pray about everything!

> The divine formula is simply this: worry about nothing, pray about everything!

When my wife, Muriel, and I were

confronted with the news that she had breast cancer, it took some days for the reality of this shocking information to sink in. We went to prayer immediately and often. We mobilized others to pray with us. Within days well over one hundred e-mails came in from people all over the world assuring us that we were in their prayers.

Apart from a few isolated anxious moments, we experienced incredible peace. Our home never did become a gloomy place. We had ample opportunity to test the truth of this promise while we waited several days for the pathology report on the biopsy, then the bone scan, and finally the state of the lymph nodes. We knew that the absence of anxiety and the presence of peace were supernatural—clearly from God. The peace we were experiencing was precisely what He had promised to give us. God's promise worked for us.

During one of our times of prayer, I shared Philippians 4:5-7 with Muriel. Perhaps for the first time ever, I noticed the connection between the command not to be anxious and the preceding declaration that *the Lord is near*. Of course He is. He is intimately near. His second coming is near. His presence is real. His nearness makes possible the zero anxiety. We know full well that if He was not intimately near, we would have been consumed with anxious thoughts.

> The result will be a peace of heart far more wonderful than the human mind can imagine.

In the situation we were facing the Lord seemed to be saying to us, "Look. I am very near to you. Don't worry. Bring this to me as a petition. The result will be a peace of heart far more wonderful than the human mind can imagine."

We can both say that the Lord is near, that He responds graciously to our petitions, and that where the anxiety would normally take up residence, the peace of God now resides. God's peace has become a "fortress" to protect us from the stress of anxiety.

INTIMACY WITH GOD AND LISTENING TO HIS VOICE

God is not silent; He speaks continuously. Ever since God created the universe, His "voice" has been heard and recognized clearly around the clock. The Scriptures abound with illustrations of God speaking or communicating with His children. He spoke directly to Adam and Eve in the Garden of Eden, to Abraham in the Ur of the Chaldees, to Moses on Mt. Sinai, and to all of the Old Testament prophets repeatedly. The apostles in the New Testament heard the guiding voice of God in their missionary endeavors.

Even in the twenty-first century, there are many who claim that God has spoken to them. I gladly include myself among those who recognize the voice of God frequently. Most often I hear Him speak from the Bible through His Holy Spirit. The question is not whether God is speaking. The bigger question is: Am I listening for His voice? Do I recognize His voice when He does speak? Are my ears cupped to listen intently for the voice of God? Am I on His wavelength?

As I live through a busy day, can I hear His voice breaking into whatever is occupying my attention at the moment? Have I learned the art of listening to God and to a visitor across the desk from me simultaneously? Like our computers that remain on line 24–7, am I "plugged in" with God continuously? When I spend time with Him, do I do all the talking, expecting God to do all of the listening? Would you not agree that it's more important for God to speak to us than for us to speak to Him?

The voice of God is more than a premonition or a hunch—both of which can steer us into the ditch. God's voice is not an emotional rush resulting in a tingle up my spine or an outbreak of goose bumps. Messages heard through a crystal ball, tea leaves, tarot cards, or an ouija board are not from almighty God. Séances, trances, and the consulting of mediums must not be viewed as God speaking to us. There are convincing counterfeit voices that masquerade as a word from the Almighty. We must learn to distinguish between the voice of God and the multitude of spurious voices clamoring for our attention. What is my basis for maintaining that Jesus' followers hear and recognize His voice? Jesus' beautiful allegory on the intimate communication between the shepherd and his sheep (see John 10:1-6) is comfortingly convincing that the voice of the Good Shepherd can be heard and recognized.

> The voice of God is more than a premonition or a hunch.

Notice first that *the sheep recognize the Shepherd's voice.* How had this intimate voice recognition developed? In the world of Near-Eastern shepherding, each shepherd had a unique voice with a unique way of speaking to his sheep. Over time the sheep became so familiar with the shepherd's voice, that whenever he spoke, they would know immediately that it was their shepherd; they would respond without hesitation. An otherwise dumb animal was most alert when its shepherd spoke. Sheep would bolt from a shepherd whose voice they did not recognize. It was hearing the voice of the shepherd repeatedly that developed this ability to recognize the shepherd's voice.

How do we recognize the voice of Jesus Christ, our Shepherd? Is it not through cultivating our listening skills or by spending time in

His presence? Is it not through hearing His voice again and again, distinguishing it from the cacophonous sounds of other voices clamoring for our attention? Is it not through spending unhurried, uninterrupted time with Him? Is it not through coming to understand what He would and would not say to us? And is it not through listening intently as He communicates with us through His eternal Word?

Second, in the Near-Eastern world of shepherding, *the shepherd knew each sheep by name.* Each sheep in his flock had a unique character. It was not only the voice of the shepherd that reassured the sheep, but also his personal attention. The shepherd led the sheep as a flock; he also led the sheep individually. When necessary, the shepherd would even carry his sheep. When ill or hurt, he would nurse the sheep. Each sheep knew that it was the object of the shepherd's tender care. What comfort there is in knowing that Jesus' treatment of us is not a "one size fits all." The way He treated the Twelve illustrates His personal touch with each of His followers. Frequently Jesus spoke with all twelve of His disciples, especially when He wanted to help them understand His public teaching more fully. What Jesus had shared with the crowds, He personalized privately and more fully with those nearer to Him. He was never too busy to spend time with the Twelve or with three, two, or just one of them. Often He pulled Peter, James, and John aside for time with just the three of them. He also spoke to Peter alone. Even Judas was given one-on-one time with Jesus.

Third, in the world of Near-Eastern shepherding, *the shepherd led his sheep; he did not drive them.* The very nature of sheep is to go astray; they cannot find their way without a shepherd. Sheep are clueless about direction. The shepherd Jesus was referring to did not have a trained sheep dog to keep the sheep in line. His intimate relationship with each of his sheep, his recognizable voice, his walking in front of them to protect and direct them, all combined to make the sheep willing to follow the shepherd to their pastures, even if it meant traversing rugged terrain. Sheep cannot find pasture on their own. They may think they can, but going their own way inevitably results in disaster.

What comfort there is in knowing that Jesus Christ, our Good Shepherd, does not drive or push us down an unfamiliar path alone. Wherever He asks us to go, He has already gone before us. We will never be the first to step onto a strange path. He beckons us to follow Him; He does not send us out to spy out the land alone. Is He sending me as a missionary to a strange land with strange people who speak a strange language and live by strange customs? When I arrive He will be there ahead of me. Is He asking me to stand before an audience to deliver His message? Then I can be sure that He will stand in that pulpit with me. I need not fear that He will abandon me to walk His chosen path alone. Never! Whenever and wherever He sends His own sheep, He goes before them.

> Wherever He asks us to go, He has already gone before us.

So then, why is it that we are willing to follow our Shepherd? It is because we recognize Jesus' voice beckoning us to follow Him. It is safe to follow Him. He does not say. "Go there!" but rather, "Take My hand and come with Me." He does not point the finger to a distant height and say, "I want you to take that hill!" No! This is not the way He treats His sheep. Instead He says, "Come with Me and together we will take that hill!"

In His application of the parable of the shepherd and his sheep, Jesus drew the following analogies to Himself:

- He is the gate to the sheepfold. He guards the flock from marauders.
- He provides abundant life for us as His sheep. He feeds the flock.
- As the Good Shepherd, He actually gives His life for the sheep. He sacrifices Himself for the flock.
- As the Good Shepherd, He recognizes His sheep and they recognize Him. He communicates intimately with the flock.
- He likens the intimacy of relationship between Himself and the

sheep to His intimate relationship to the Father. He also describes His intimate relationship with us as eternal.

There is one more beautiful lesson in Jesus' teaching on the shepherd and the sheep; it is the lesson of the *other sheep* not yet in Jesus' fold. Jesus was looking into the future and anticipating the day when the Gentile world would hear His voice and become part of His "flock of sheep." Jesus' "other sheep" strategy fits perfectly into His mission to seek and to save the lost. He says that these other sheep will also hear His voice. Think of it! The same joy we share recognizing the voice of our loving Shepherd will be experienced by sheep of every tongue, tribe, kindred, and nation.

Today God's voice will come to us in these reliable ways:

- The Holy Spirit speaking to us as we spend time reading, meditating, studying, and obeying the Scriptures
- The Holy Spirit nudging or prompting us to bring our words, deeds, thoughts, attitudes, and motivations into alignment with the eternal truths in the Word of God
- The Holy Spirit convicting us of a sin to confess or a broken relationship to mend
- The Holy Spirit sharing a helpful word of encouragement, exhortation, or rebuke through a Christian brother or sister
- The Holy Spirit impressing on our hearts the will of God regarding His day-to-day lifelong purposes.

INTIMACY WITH GOD AND OBEDIENCE

While staying overseas in a guest house, I took time to reflect on my personal obedience to God. The result was the following piece in one of my e-mails to Muriel:

> *Muriel, as I reflected on my own obedience to God today, these thoughts came to me. I pray that they will bless you and that together we will go deeper in our submission to God. Of course, Jesus is our example. His prayers were heard by the Father because of His reverent submission, and although He was a son, He learned obedience from what He suffered (see Hebrews 5:7-8). Think of it! "Reverent submission." "Learned obedience." Amazing! The omnipotent One submitting and the omniscient One learning obedience. If this was a lesson Jesus had to learn, what makes me think that I'll master it easily? I'm set to remain in obedience school all my days!*

> Obedience brings pleasure to my Master and leads me more intimately into His presence.

Jesus faced the ultimate test of obedience in the Garden of Gethsemane. There He actually prayed that if the Father's will would allow bypassing the cross, He would rather take that path, but the bottom line for Jesus was always His Father's plan (see Matthew 26:42; Luke 22:42). Fulfilling His purpose must be my ultimate goal too. Obedience brings pleasure to my Master and leads me more intimately into His presence. Over these many years of learning obedience, I do not recall regretting even one such act of submission. My only regret is that there were times when my, "Yes, Lord, I'll do it!" wasn't more immediate and enthusiastic.

I can still hear our children and now our grandchildren ask the "why" questions. I can also remember an occasional response something like, "Simply because I asked you to do so." You and I had both the right and the responsibility to ask our children to obey. In those days our children were in the process of learning obedience and trust. We are still in a similar process with God. We knew that the most important lesson we could teach our children was obedience. Is it any different for our heavenly Father? In cases where the love of a patient parent or the willful waywardness of a child do not lead to obedience, the heavier, harsher hand of the law may have to intervene. Similarly, we force God to resort to more painful means when we refuse to obey, perhaps like a shepherd who breaks the leg of a straying sheep and then nurses it back to wholeness.

Obedience to God must be immediate, complete, joyful, and lifelong— no bargaining, no complaints, and no delays. We need not know why God is asking us to do a certain thing. Persisting with the "why" questions may be nothing more than an unconscious attempt to change God's mind, to suggest that we have a better plan, or worse, outright rebellion against Him. All we need is to be clear on just the initial step in what He asks of us. It's not likely that He will show us the entire path, for a life of obedience is also a faith journey. The day may come when we know the "why," but then again, we may never know this side of eternity. We must beware of insisting on answers to the "why" question as a precondition to obedience. Even our closest, most godly friends *may* not have answers for us. Usually, God reserves them for Himself. When it comes to matters of obedience to God, we must beware of seeking out the counsel we want to hear. It's possible to fortify willfulness by searching out agreeable counsel, counsel that does not come from God.

The divine agenda behind the call to obedience may be no more than a test to see if we will indeed follow Jesus. Submission to the lordship of Jesus Christ may indeed have an initial, dramatic starting point, but thereafter it's a matter of daily acts of obedience, both big and small, public and private. To obey God without knowing the reason why may seem like a blind leap into the dark, but this is where my trust and devotion to Him comes in. There are also times when obedience is toward leaders God has placed over me (see Hebrews 13:17). As a leader, I can expect the same level of respect I give to leaders over me.

> To obey God without knowing the reason why . . . is where my trust and devotion to Him comes in.

Do I really think I could outdo the God who created the universe with all of its intricate detail and its mind-boggling infinities and come up with a better plan? Has He not proved Himself faithful in the past? If so, why should I begin to doubt Him now? Has there ever been even one instance where He has failed me? Since there isn't, what grounds do I have for thinking He would begin to do so now? Has He ever steered me into a ditch or led me astray? This would be totally out of character for Him who never ceases to watch over me. Has He ever given me anything but a good gift? Even our earthly fathers do not give us a stone or a scorpion when we ask for bread or fish. I may guess at why He is asking me to obey Him in a certain matter, but to press too hard for answers now may rob me of the joy of divine disclosure in His time. The absolute beauty and rightness of His plan will then dawn on me, causing my soul to exclaim, "Thank God I had the sense to obey Him," and at the same time, shudder over the disastrous results of following my own inferior plan.

What a risk God takes when He allows me to choose between His perfect way and my own flawed plans. Again, the ultimate reasons why God is asking me to embark on a certain path may not be apparent till we step into eternity. No matter, for the day will certainly come when I will comprehend the full extent to which the will of God is good, acceptable, and perfect. In a million years of toil, I could not come up with even one plan as perfect as His. The beautiful fruit of obedience is to discover the perfect will of God.

INTIMACY WITH GOD AND WEAKNESS

J esus said to Paul, *"My grace is sufficient for you, for my power is made perfect in weakness.'* Paul responded, *"Therefore, I will boast all the more gladly about my weaknesses, so that Christ's power may rest on me. That is why, for Christ's sake, I delight in weaknesses, in insults, in hardships, in persecutions, in difficulties. For when I am weak, then I am strong" (2 Corinthians 12:9-10).*

One of my most vivid early teen memories is joining my dad and the other farmers at J.C. Neufeldt's country store. The only other public building in Capasin was my one-room country schoolhouse where thirteen of us made up the entire student body.

At the store, I heard tales of physical prowess that held me spellbound. I still remember the account of the poor farmer who was given a hundred-pound bag of flour on condition that he could carry it to his house a mile away. (I never did find out if he made it!) At times, there were wrist-wrestling matches. I was particularly pleased watching my father win many of these contests. In the prime of life, he was physically strong, and I admired him for it. In retrospect, I suspect that some of the stories I heard were somewhat embellished. Nevertheless, I grew up with a high degree of respect and admiration for physical strength and disdain for any kind of weakness. My heroes were these macho men, the ones with bulging muscles, and those who were sharpshooters with their rifles. They could rope and brand steers, tame wild horses, and fell tall trees with their double bitted axes. I was well on my way to becoming like them.

Little wonder I enjoyed reading the account of David's mighty men and their amazing exploits. First, there was Jashobeam who single-handedly took out three hundred enemy soldiers with his sword. There was also Eleazar who turned to face the enemy when others fled in retreat and turned a rout into a resounding victory. Then there was Benaiah who took on two seasoned enemy warriors and killed them both, went into a snowy pit and killed a lion, and faced an armed Egyptian Goliath-like giant with a club and killed him. It is not surprising that David chose Benaiah to be his personal bodyguard.

Over the years, my perspective has changed greatly. Yes, I enjoyed watching Lance Armstrong's repeated Tour de France victories or Steve Fawcett's solo flight around the world in a balloon. The very memory of standing on top of Mt. Popocatepetl near Mexico City after an arduous climb still exhilarates my whole being. Today, however, my greatest thrill is seeing someone with severe limitations far exceed the best that man can do, not through his own strength and determination, but through the sufficient grace of God. Although unnoticed by many, their achievements break all records and bring gladness to the heart of almighty God.

The apostle Paul is such a person. To keep him humble over some of the ecstatic spiritual experiences God had given him as well as the unusual celestial visions God had allowed him to see, God arranged for a severe trial, a trial that may have been physically debilitating. At the very least, his "thorn in the flesh" placed severe limitations on him. We can only guess at the actual nature of the "thorn." It may have simply been the aging process coupled with arthritis. Others have suggested that his "thorn in the flesh" was epilepsy, chronic ophthalmia, or recurring bouts of malaria. In any case, it is difficult to imagine continuing an itinerant ministry or long periods in a prison cell or dungeon with a limiting physical malady.

So, the great apostle who had seen God answer numerous personal prayers in dramatic and miraculous ways, prayed to God for healing. His full expectation seemed to be that God would indeed heal him. Paul's prayers for deliverance from his "thorn" were not some by-the-way, off-the-cuff kind of prayers. On three distinct occasions, Paul made his "thorn in the flesh" a matter of fervent, importunate prayer.

The Lord Jesus Christ personally delivered the answer to Paul's prayer. What Jesus said to Paul was not what he expected. In essence, Jesus' answer to Paul's plea was as follows: *"I will not remove your 'thorn in the flesh;' instead, I will give you enough of My grace to cope with your malady, and further, I will make of you an exhibit of My overcoming power."* Jesus' answer to Paul's prayer continues to help all of us to this very day. This is because we have prayed similar prayers and received similar answers. God may choose to heal us, change a trying circumstance, remove or transfer an impossible person, or He may choose to leave the troubling situation as it is but give us sufficient grace to cope with it victoriously.

All of us have preconceived notions about the best way for God to answer our prayers. Of course, healing us when sick would be best, or so we think. A change in my circumstances would be most helpful, or so it seems at present. Moreover, having so-and-so taken out of my life would clearly be the best solution, but God may have a much better remedy. God's solution always has in it the greatest good, for the largest number of people, and for the greatest length of time. Furthermore, whatever God's response to our

> All of us have preconceived notions about the best way for God to answer our prayers.

prayer for the removal of our "thorn in the flesh" is, we can be sure that it will be accompanied by His grace and power.

Which is a greater demonstration of God's power, to heal us instantly or to give us the daily strength to press on joyfully? A healing might bring with it short-term amazement and elation, whereas persevering day after day may well move more people to inquire about the source of such genuine, supernatural joy. The sufficient grace of God in the midst of a severe trial is most attractive—attractive because it models an intimate walk with God.

Which is the greater victory, to have a difficult person "transferred" or to have God grant an infusion of patience to endure cheerfully? A "transfer" does little for the one removed, but being treated with cheerful patience may lead him to ask about your source of patience. It is the sufficient grace of God putting up with a difficult person that is so attractive—attractive because it advertises the sufficiency of God's grace; further, it models an intimate walk with God.

Which is the greater triumph, to have a trying circumstance changed or to be given eyes to see the good it will bring to us and to others if it remains as it is? Living above the difficult circumstance will make a greater impact than having it changed. It is the sufficient grace of God in the midst of a trying circumstance that is very attractive—attractive because it points to the power of God in the midst of a test; it also models an intimate walk with God.

> God delights to help the helpless.

The world insists, "God helps those who help themselves." Nothing could be further from the truth. God delights to help the helpless. He pays special attention to the weak. He is nearest to those who need Him. As a pure pearl displayed on black velvet accenting its beauty, the child of God exhibits the sufficiency and beauty of God's power at the very point of our weakness. We must choose between our own self-sufficiency and God's sufficient grace. If we insist on the former, we forfeit the latter.

How could Paul actually "boast" in his weakness? We must understand that he did not rejoice in his "thorn in the flesh" as such, but he did exult in the power of Christ unleashed by the "thorn."

Paul could "delight" in weaknesses simply because in that state he could be strong in Christ. After receiving assurance of God's grace and power, he ceased asking God to remove the "thorn in the flesh." He gladly accepted Jesus' answer as the superior solution. Experiencing the grace and power of God in the midst of his ongoing limitations was better by far than having the "thorn" removed.

Every servant of God feels weak in the face of his/her God-given assignments. Who is sufficient for a God-sized mission? Who has not objected when God called? Who has not felt like running away like Jonah did. When God called Jeremiah, he complained that he could not speak and that he was only a child. God's response was most assuring: "Jeremiah, do not be afraid because I am going to be with you and will rescue you."

When God called Moses to lead His people out of Egypt, he insisted that he "had never been eloquent" and that he was "slow of speech." At his point of weakness, God assured him with, "I will help you speak and will teach you what to say." God delights in choosing the weakest, the most unlikely of His children, and makes of them an exhibit of His grace and power. Have we not all wondered how it was that certain ones were chosen to take on major leadership responsibilities? God chose them because they recognized their personal deficits.

To tap into the grace and power of God, we must acknowledge our weakness. We must learn the secret of drawing on His grace and power where we are weakest. The less I have in myself, the more I am compelled to rely on Him. The less I have in myself, the more room there is for His grace and power.

The link between intimacy with God and our weakness is clear. As often as we come to the Lord and say, "Faithful Father, this is too big for me, this is too difficult for me, this is over my head," that's how often He draws near and whispers, "It's not too big for me; leave it to me. Here, put your hand in mine and we'll do it together. My grace is always enough for every trial."

INTIMACY WITH GOD
AND REVIVAL

This is what the high and lofty One says—he who lives forever, whose name is holy: "I live in a high and holy place, but also with him who is contrite and lowly in spirit, to revive the spirit of the lowly and to revive the heart of the contrite." (Isaiah 57:15, emphasis added)

During a visit to the northwest corner of the Democratic Republic of Congo (DRC), I made a wonderful discovery. In August of 1951, the Holy Spirit visited that region known as the Ubangi with spiritual revival. I had heard of this revival, but by March of 2004, the time of my visit, this event had become but a faint footnote in my memory. This was about to change with the listening to many memories of the Ubangi Revival.

The occasion of my visit to the Ubangi was to help celebrate the eighty-second anniversary of our sister church. Given my interest in Church Planting Movements (CPM), I decided to interview as many African leaders as possible to find out what are the marks of a CPM leader. Ann Wester was designated to be my interpreter into either French or Lingala.

Without me even asking about the revival in 1951, pastor after pastor made reference to it, especially the older local church pastors. Almost all of the twenty-five interviews gave some further information about the "showers of blessing" that fell on the Ubangi in 1951 for upwards of two years. Some of the older pastors, now in their eighties, became animated with joyous excitement as they shared their memories.

Though the impact of the spiritual renewal was waning some fifty years later, most of the leaders of our one-hundred-thousand-member-strong sister church view the decade of the fifties as the golden era of the Congo church. Many of the pastors are praying fervently and frequently that the Holy Spirit would once again graciously lead the church, which is much larger now, through another revival.

> God looks for one or a few people who have humble and contrite hearts.

How did the revival start? In the histories of spiritual awakenings, there is no exception to the classic starting points. They seem always to be present. The pattern seems something like this: God looks for one or a few people who have humble and contrite hearts. He gives them the gift of repentance and places on their hearts an intense desire for intimacy with the Almighty. They see the exceeding holiness of God and at the same time the blackness of their own sinfulness and unworthiness. The pure holiness of God and the utter sinfulness of man lead to intense prayer for God's mercy, forgiveness, and cleansing. Frequently it is the sin of coldness, indifference, or apathy that is confessed to God.

News of the Billy Graham Crusade in Los Angeles impacted the prayer life of the missionaries in the Ubangi serving with the EFCA International Mission. Since the Spirit of God had graciously visited the Graham Crusade in distant America, could He not do the same in Congo? Of course He could! The missionaries began to pray. The focus of all meetings, regardless of their agenda, began to be prayer for revival. This included Mission Council meetings, meetings with medical staff, and meetings with high school and primary school teachers. Accompanying long periods of prayer, sometimes from early in the morning till well into the night, was confession of specific sin and humbly asking for forgiveness—missionary-to-missionary, missionary-to-national worker. Many marriages were strengthened during the Ubangi revival.

As closely as I can piece the information on the revival together, it had its genesis at the Bau mission station. Free Church missionary Clarence Lundberg, influenced by the Billy Graham Crusades in Los Angeles, began to pray for revival in the Ubangi. He asked a young African Bible Institute graduate, John Mobaya, to join him in prayer for revival. The two of them teamed up to fast and pray for revival for the better part of a week in Mobaya's village house. Thereafter, it seems, the two of them as well as others traveled to meetings from station-to-station and village-to-village preaching powerfully on "sin and Jesus." James 4:7-10 proved to be the text for many of the messages preached during the Ubangi Revival: "Submit to God! Resist the Devil! Come near to God! Purify your hearts! Grieve, mourn, and wail! Humble yourselves before the Lord and He will lift you up!"

When the Holy Spirit visits Christ's church with revival, He is also in charge of the schedule, the program, and the manifestations. These cannot be dictated to Him. The Holy Spirit is the gracious Orchestrator of every spiritual awakening. Here are some of marks of the Ubangi Revival:

- In 1951 the church in the Ubangi was small and overtaken by a sense of hopelessness on the part of some and coldness in others. There was tension among the missionaries and nationals. The teaching of important doctrines seemed to fall on deaf ears. It seems now that the church in the Ubangi had fallen into a state of spiritual impotence. There was known sin in the lives of workers who were living a double life.
- There was a hunger and thirst for holiness on the part of some; they cried out to God for cleansing and forgiveness.

- A decision was made on the part of missionaries to look for like-hearted Africans and invite them to join in prayer for revival.
- One of the phenomena of the Ubangi Revival was the spontaneous and simultaneous congregational prayers. The urgency to confess sin to God was so great that all prayed at once. Tears of repentance wet the dirt floors in the churches. Whole congregations prayed on their knees or prostrate on the dirt floor, but all were confessing their sins to God.
- Missionaries seemed willing to go into their annual conference without a schedule or agenda. Instead of the usual printed program, they waited upon the Holy Spirit to direct them. God gave just the right messages when needed.
- He also gave a desire to pray by the hour.
- Believers getting right with one another had a profound impact on the surrounding pagan community.
- Unbelievers brought their fetishes, amulets, and other spirit worship paraphernalia, piled them in a heap, and burned them as a sign of their new allegiance to Jesus Christ.

The revival in the Ubangi gave birth to new mission stations. Many teams of evangelists and preachers traveled more widely with the gospel than ever before. Some of the most influential, effective, and powerful pastors received their call to full-time service during the revival. Not only was the church energized during this time of revival, it ensured strong, godly leaders in the years ahead. Some say that the revival

> Every believer can live in a state of continuous revival.

also prepared the church in the Ubangi for the terrible upheavals that engulfed the entire nation in the sixties.

Why have I chosen to speak of revival in this series of essays on intimacy with God? My personal conviction on this matter is that individually, *every believer can live in a state of continuous revival.* This is God's desire for His children. Our faithful Father has put at the disposal of His children all of the resources needed to keep fanning the flames of personal revival. I see personal revival and intimacy with God as one and the same. Desiring God, delighting in God, and seeking after God all contribute toward a state of personal revival as well as to an intimate walk with God. I noticed heart-hunger and soul-thirst among missionaries and African co-workers. God has promised to satisfy our hunger and quench our thirst. The daily practice of confession of sin to God and communion with God enhance intimacy with Him. Such practices also fuel the fires of personal revival.

The revival in the Ubangi went much beyond personal renewal; it set entire congregations, communities, and even regions ablaze with zeal for God. The Ubangi Pentecost, as some call it, revived an entire church movement. It is my contention that every Church Planting Movement must encounter the power of God through a sweeping revival at least once a generation. If it does not, it will slip to the level of a spiritually dead and impotent organization. Had the Holy Spirit not revived the Ubangi church in 1951, it may well not have survived the cataclysmic upheavals of the sixties.

I said good-bye to the leaders of the church in the Ubangi with a commitment to pray for revival, not only in the Ubangi, but in each place we seek to plant churches or see them renewed. Come, Holy Spirit, revive Your church.

INTIMACY WITH GOD AND THE "WITH HIM" PRINCIPLE

The concept I speak of here doubles as both an intimacy with God principle and as a ministry principle. This should not surprise us since intimacy with God and service for God are inextricably linked together. During our church-planting years in Malaysia, Mark 3:14 became a key text in my relationship with the church-planting teams I was training. I go so far as to say that the Mark account of Jesus calling His disciples revolutionized my approach to church planting. Rather than looking for volunteers to help me with this and that in my church-planting ministry, I prayed fervently for a team of committed men and women, a team that made the commitment to plant a church with me.

> Intimacy with God and service for God are inextricably linked together.

During the church-planting process, my personal focus was the teaching, training, and mentoring of the team of national lay workers. The results were most gratifying. Rather than plant the church around my few gifts and my limited experience, the new church plant reaped the benefit of all of the gifts of the entire team. From the outset, the DNA of these team-led church plants was strongly Asian and not Western. I knew that the day would come when I would have to leave the church plant behind. I was determined that I would leave behind a team of strong leaders.

This did not mean that I wasn't involved in the ministries that go into planting a new church. I was deeply involved in praying, evangelizing, teaching, planning, modeling, etc., but always with or through the team and rarely alone. I met with the team two evenings a week to do more of the formal training, but the equipping ministry was not limited to these regularly scheduled meetings. I was seeking to put Jesus' "with-Him" principle into practice. This meant spending an enormous amount of time with the members of the team both individually and collectively, formally and informally. It also meant living a much more transparent life than during my days as a solo church planter.

After Jesus had spent the night praying to the Father (see Luke 6:12ff), He chose and appointed the Twelve. What was His initial reason for appointing His followers? It was simply that they might be "with Him." In due time they would go out to preach; they would also be given authority to demonstrate the power of God. But for three years they were to be with Jesus to observe Him, to listen to Him, to learn from Him, to understand His agenda, and most importantly, come to understand who Jesus was. They were to spend much time in the presence of Jesus in every conceivable life situation. We might even say that they spent an enormous amount of time simply "hanging out" with Jesus. They were to be transformed by Jesus' teaching and by His life. We may wonder why the Great Commission was not accompanied by clear step-by-step instructions on how to make disciples. This was not necessary since Jesus had shown His followers how to make disciples over a period of years. He did not write a manual on disciple-making tips. Instead He modeled disciple making for the Twelve. Illustrations of the "with-Him" principle, or of the "Mark 3:14 Moments," abound in the four gospel accounts. Although it is true that Jesus ministered to the masses, His twelve disciples were His priority.

Frequently after speaking to the crowds with His disciples forming the immediate circle around Him, He bade the multitudes farewell and took the Twelve aside for deeper teaching. The following sampling of the "Mark 3:14 Moments" make clear that Jesus' strategy was to personally equip His disciples before sending them out in obedience to the Great Commission. He asked them to follow Him before He sent them out to make disciples of all nations.

- *"When he was alone with his own disciples, he explained everything"* (Mark 4:34).
- *"After he had left the crowd and entered the house, his disciples asked him about this parable"* (Mark 7:17).
- *"When they were in the house again, the disciples asked Jesus about this"* (Mark 10:10).
- *"Again he took the Twelve aside and told them what was going to happen to him"* (Mark 10:32).

I hasten to say that any of us attempting to implement the "with-Him" principle must also confess our limitations. We are not Jesus. We are more like the members of Jesus' team. Nevertheless, Jesus gave us a permanent ministry principle to emulate. As stated above, I see in the "Mark 3:14 Moments" in the gospels both a strategy for ministry and a principle that enhances an intimate walk with God. The ministry principle in Jesus' "with-Him" example is not difficult to understand. To train the Twelve, Jesus invested time to be with them. It is no different for us. All of the technology in the world will not provide us with a shortcut to maturity. Maturity comes through observing and imitating those who are mature. Let's now look briefly at the other side of the "with-Him" principle that points us in the direction of intimacy with God.

We already know that intimacy with God begins with spending time with Jesus before we go out into the world to bring the lost to the feet of the Savior. The order must be this: time with Jesus to become like

Him followed by time with the people to tell them about Him. We take on the likeness of those with whom we spend time. To take on the likeness of Jesus is the most effective way to engage in fruitful evangelism. We must "see" His beauty, "hear" His voice, and submit to His teaching before we can

> We take on the likeness of those with whom we spend time.

convince even one person to become His follower. It is a tragic mistake to think that we can bypass private communion with Jesus and go directly into the public arena of ministry.

Interestingly, the presence of Jesus was so strong on the disciples after His ascension, that the religious establishment *"took note that these men* [Peter and John] *had been with Jesus"* (Acts 4:13). Whether the people we serve can articulate their sense of Jesus in us as clearly as the religious rulers did of Peter and John or not, there will be something compelling about what we have to say. Communion with God or practicing intimacy with God becomes the fountainhead or the wellspring of all of our service for God.

Recently I had an e-mail exchange with one of our workers on this very topic. I wrote:

Your response to my brief note blessed me very much. You said: "I have been especially experiencing the joy of being with Jesus, and then with people." I responded as follows: *That is precisely the order in which intimacy with God and the ministry of evangelism should take place. Evangelism is really the overflow of times of communion with God. It is difficult (probably impossible) to speak warmly and convincingly of Jesus when He seems distant.*

INTIMACY WITH GOD AND SILENCE

"Be still, and know that I am God; I will he exalted among the nations, I will be exalted in the earth." (Psalm 46:10)

Consider this paraphrase of God's personal word to us about silence, about knowing Him, and about His sovereign control over the nations: "Hush! Put the brakes on your pell-mell pace! Stop, look, and listen! Let Me remind you that I really am in control and that My plan A always works. I have never had to resort to plan B. Allow Me to flood your soul with the assurance that one day all the nations on earth will bow down before Me."

> Where does almighty God fit into a noisy world like ours?

This world is indeed a clamorous, demanding place. Our ears must cope with ever-higher decibels, our eyes with more rapidfire images on television, and our minds with a relentless barrage of data from the media. An overstatement? For most working people this is raw reality. Overload? For many it is.

Where does almighty God fit into a noisy world like ours? Must He make an appointment, take a number, or sit in the waiting room outside our office with everyone else? How tragic to come to the end of a day only to remember that we stood Him up in our early morning appointment for a time of silent communion with Him? Throughout the day there was hardly a God-conscious thought. "Sorry, Lord," we say with bone-weary exhaustion before falling into bed, "perhaps I'll do better tomorrow."

The fruit of such a pace is a shallow, unsatisfying relationship with God, an emptiness of soul, and a longing for something deeper, something much more. If you are like me, you know instinctively that such emptiness has everything to do with my relationship with God. If only I could establish an intimate, satisfying, fulfilling relationship with God Almighty, everything else would begin to fall into place. That's the key. We know in our heart of hearts that this is so.

We also know instinctively and from experience that an intimate walk with God cannot be nourished by an occasional on-the-run conversation with Him. What will it take? It will take disciplined determination to set aside a block of quality time for communion with God before the day begins—not occasionally, but daily. Seven out of seven! It will take getting up before our noisy, unreasonable world does. It will take making my "quiet time" with God my lifelong priority. My early appointment with God must be regarded as more important than sleep itself.

Spending time in unhurried, uninterrupted communion with God must come before conversations with others, before checking the sports scores in the daily newspaper, before breakfast, and before the *Good Morning America* news hour. Time with God can totally change the demanding day ahead; it sets the tone for the day before it even begins. As Francis de Sales writes in *Introduction to the Devout Life*: "Just as the firefly passes through flames without burning its wings, so also a strong, resolute soul can live in the world without being infected by any of its moods, find sweet springs of piety amid its salty waves. . ."

The overflow of the "be-still-and-know" time with God will irrigate the soul throughout the most demanding day. A time of quiet in the presence of God early in the morning is a bit like booting up a computer, logging onto the Internet, and remaining online all day long. From that time of communion with God before the day begins, we can carry His presence into every conversation, every decision, and every meeting. He, in turn, can break into our day repeatedly with thoughts, words, reminders, and ideas that help our situations. The child of God who has listened to the voice of God in the morning will also hear His voice throughout the day. For the Christian, the equivalent to booting up, logging on, and remaining online all day is that essential time of communion with the Father, Son, and Holy Spirit at the outset of the day.

"Be still. . ." The command to be still (silent) is not an easy one to obey. Silence seems totally out-of-step with the pervasive restlessness in our society. But it is a command, and God does not ask anything of us He does not also help us with. Initially silence in His presence will seem awkward. We have an almost irresistible urge to fill the silence with words or at least with some background music.

Why does God command silence? Simply because He has a lot to say to us. Silence gives us perspective, God's perspective. Silence brings our thoughts and motivations into alignment with God's ways. Silence allows the Holy Spirit to nudge us, to prompt us in the direction of the Father's eternal purposes. During times of silence the Spirit of God can outline a clear course of action for us. He can "write'" vision, direction, and game plans on the "tablet" of our heart. It is during times of silence that we receive our assignments from God. This is also when we either learn the will of God or have it confirmed. My Lord and I can alternate speaking and listening. This makes for the most delightful of conversations. Just think of it! My Lord Jesus and I listening and speaking with each other!

Normally, the quietest time is in the middle of the night. We may fret over not being able to sleep at 2:00 a.m. Instead of anxiety over the sleep we are missing, realize that it may well be our heavenly Father awakening us for a time of communion. David spoke of searching his heart while in bed; he also spoke of tears in the night as he reflected on his sin (see

Psalm 4:4, 6:6). We all know the account of God calling Samuel three times in the middle of the night (1 Samuel 3:10). God chose the quiet of the night to reveal His plan for Israel's future. I have come to view time awake as an opportunity to pray, to search my heart, and to worship the living God. I attribute an intensified desire for an intimate walk with God to a time of communion with my Lord in the middle of the night while in Moscow in December of 1996.

"Be still and know . . ." The order is important. It is stillness before discovery, silence before knowing. If we really want to hear the voice of God, we must listen before Him in silence. If we really want to understand His perfect will and know His holy character, we must learn how to be silent in His presence. Our many words drown out His voice. We are a wordy people living in a wordy world, but in God's plan for intimacy with Him, there are

> We listen when we meditate and reflect on God's Word in the Bible.

times when we must listen while He speaks. Think for a moment how much we miss if we keep prattling on! We have said repeatedly that it is more important for God to speak to us than for us to speak to God. This being so also means that it is more important for us to develop the art of listening to God than the skill of speaking to God. We listen when we meditate and reflect on God's Word in the Bible. This is where God speaks most clearly and most powerfully. There are times, however, when silence means no activity whatsoever. It may simply be with eyes closed, open hands spread out expectantly to our faithful Father, knees bent, head bowed, heart yielded, and will submitted to the triune God. Our only words are, "Speak Lord, I am listening."

"Be still and know that I am God." God has so much to teach us about Himself. Here in our text He wants us to know that He and not another is the one true God; He is the eternally existing I AM. All the other gods are not gods. He wants us also to know that He is sovereignly in control

of our immediate little world as well as of our big global world. The time will come when all the peoples of the world will recognize Him as their Creator and as their Savior. They will fall on their knees and confess with their mouth that Jesus Christ is Lord.

Every missionary must take encouragement in the certainty of God's promise. There is no question but that all the nations of the world will acknowledge and exalt our sovereign Lord as the one and only Jehovah God. Isaiah 11:9 is a prophetic promise similar to the one given to us through the prophet Habakkuk: *"The earth will be filled with the knowledge of the glory of the LORD, as the waters cover the sea"* (Habakkuk 2:14). Every missionary must also be reminded that God's eternal plans, God's lofty ways, and His deepest desires are revealed in times of being silent in His presence.

INTIMACY WITH GOD AND WALKING WITH GOD

A re you searching for an intimate walk with God to imitate? In Holy Scripture Enoch's example of intimacy with God is among the finest. He lived just seven generations after Adam, the first man created by God. Adam was still alive when Enoch was born to his father Jared. Because Enoch's time on earth overlapped with Adam, he was able to introduce his son Methuselah to his elderly ancestor.

Other patriarchs listed in Enoch's family tree were born, lived some years before they fathered children, and then lived additional years before they died. This tedious cycle of life, birth, and death continued generation after generation.

When Enoch came onto the scene, he broke this monotonous cycle by establishing an intimate relationship with God. Twice we are told that Enoch *walked with God.* Enoch's most important life achievement was his intimate relationship with God. Only two other men in Genesis had such a reputation; they were Noah, Enoch's great-grandson, and Abraham.

What does it mean to walk with God? Surely, it is more than a sentimental hand-in-hand stroll in the meadows. To walk with God means to be in agreement with Him, to have my thoughts and attitudes in alignment with His. To walk with God means to obey Him, to trust

Him, and to live in harmony with Him. It is not possible for two to walk together intimately apart from total agreement with each other.

Enoch made it into the Hebrews 11 "Hall of Faith." To be listed in Hebrews 11 is like being buried in Arlington Cemetery with a twenty-one-gun salute! Only those who have achieved exploits of faith appear in the Christian Hall of Faith. Enoch is there. Interestingly, he and Noah are the only ones from the Genesis 5 genealogy to make it into God's Hall of Faith.

There is a third mention of Enoch in the Scriptures. Jude, the brother of Jesus and of James, tells us about Enoch's public prophetic preaching ministry (Jude 14, 15). In this, Noah followed in the footsteps of his great-grandfather Enoch, for Noah too was a "preacher of righteousness."

Enoch's intimate walk with God leaves us a rich legacy of life lessons. The Spirit of God moved three different biblical writers to include these few snapshots from Enoch's life. They are included in the Bible for these instructions:

Walking Intimately with God Has a Beginning

We do not accidentally slide into an intimate walk with God. Most of us can recall the circumstances around which our hunger for God intensified, a time when nothing mattered as much as an intimate walk with God. For Enoch the starting point seems to have been the birth of his son, Methuselah. God uses a variety of events, circumstances, and experiences to draw us close to His side— marriage, the birth of a child, an illness, a death, a divorce in the family, a failure, or a success. Wherever we observe an intimate walk with God, we can be sure that God Himself initiated it. He stimulates and satisfies our heart hunger; He stirs and quenches our soul thirst. Left

> God uses a variety of events, circumstances, and experiences to draw us close to His side.

to ourselves we would be content to live a humdrum existence like the other generations in Enoch's family tree. God mercifully draws us out of the low life onto a higher plane.

Walking Intimately with God Is Possible in an Indifferent, Ungodly Society

There is no record of anyone else in Enoch's day walking intimately with God. He is singled out as the only one. That Enoch walked alone with God should not surprise us. Just as eagles do not fly in flocks, it is unlikely that you will ever join a crowd of Christians pursuing an intimate walk with God. Thankfully, we do encounter a fellow traveler on a similar quest here and there, but for the most part it will be a journey with God alone. In spite of the decadence in the society all around him, and in spite of his hard-hitting message of judgment against the ungodly and their ungodly deeds, Enoch found time to nurture an intimate walk with God. He did not succumb to the downward pull of evil around him. He dared to be different. We cannot excuse ourselves from a diligent pursuit of intimacy with God because the world around us is falling apart. Our faithful Father's outstretched arms are calling us to turn our backs on the world and to come closer and closer to Him.

Walking Intimately with God Impacts Future Generations

It is amazing to me how much Noah was like his great-grandfather. Like Enoch, Noah had the reputation that he walked with God. Like Enoch, Noah thundered words of judgment in his preaching. Like Enoch, Noah pleased God. Did Noah set out to imitate his great-grandfather Enoch? That seems to be the case. We must never underestimate the impact our walk with God has on our children, teenagers, nieces and nephews, and grandsons and

> An intimate walk with God cannot be hidden.

granddaughters—in short, the next generation and the next and even the next after that. An intimate walk with God cannot be hidden. It will be noticed and remembered. Its impact will live on and on. Those who follow us in future generations will imitate our intimate walk with God.

Walking Intimately with God Pleases Him

Enoch was a God-pleaser; he brought joy and gladness to the heart of God. This is the part about Enoch's walk with God I like most, for I too long to please Him. God's smile of approval rested on Enoch. Enoch brought pleasure and gladness to God's heart. The two of them walked together so much and for so long that God simply took Enoch into His presence permanently. Enoch and God reveled in each other's company. An intimate walk with God is not a one-way street with God standing by watching me derive pleasure from my communion with Him. Not at all! Intimacy with God includes both of us listening and speaking to each other, both of us delighting in each other's presence, and both of us bringing boundless joy to each other.

Walking Intimately with *God* Is a Walk of Faith

This, I believe, is the primary lesson we have to learn from Enoch's intimate walk with God. Apart from a robust faith in God for every detail of every day, an intimate walk with God is an impossibility. He made it into the Hall of Faith because of his unwavering faith in God. Specifically, it was his strong faith in God that brought gladness to God's heart.

Each day that Enoch came into God's presence, he exercised faith. His life was a life of faith. His relationship with God was a faith relationship. Enoch did not see God with his physical eyes any more than we do. He may not have heard the voice of God with his physical ears either. His eyes and ears had the same limitations ours do. When we approach God, the *eyes of faith* must take over for our physical eyes. *Our faith eyes* "see" that God exists. *Faith eyes* spot frequent God-sightings where others see nothing. *Faith eyes* go beyond "Faith 101" that believes in the existence of God. *Faith eyes* fill the soul with an expectant assurance that God will reward us with an intimate relationship.

The writer to the Hebrews does not say that it is merely difficult to please God without faith. It certainly is difficult, but it is more serious than that. He states categorically that it is *impossible* to please God without faith. God seeks the pleasure of our faith.

> God seeks the pleasure of our faith.

Jesus commended faith wherever He encountered it—the faith of the Gentile centurion on behalf of his servant, the faith of the woman who was bleeding for twelve years, the faith of the two blind men asking that their sight be restored, and the Canaanite woman's faith beseeching Jesus to cast a demon out of her daughter. Most of Jesus' condemnation for a lack of faith was leveled against His own disciples (see Matthew 14:31, 16:8, 17:17). Jesus looked for and even longed for faith in His followers. Nothing has changed; He craves our implicit, childlike faith.

In summary, what do we learn about an intimate walk with God in Enoch's life? I must allow God to use the circumstances in my life to draw me into an intimate walk with Him. I must not despair if I am all alone in the pursuit of intimacy with God and no one joins me. I may not see the impact of my close walk with God, but I can rest assured that it will be there even to future generations. Finally, I must allow my *faith eyes* to develop an expectant assurance that God will indeed reward all who pursue Him with diligence. What is the reward for such a quest? It is intimacy with almighty God.